In Search *of* Blessings

In Search *of* Blessings

Kathryn Kuhlman

Bridge-Logos

Newberry, FL 32669 USA

Bridge-Logos

Newberry, FL 32669 USA

In Search of Blessings
by Kathryn Kuhlman

Copyright © 1989 by The Kathryn Kuhlman Foundation
Reprinted 2005, 2008

Printed in the United States of America.

Library of Congress Catalog Card Number: 91-78260
International Standard Book Number: 978-0-88270-869-0

BP 10-20-16

Contents

Biography

Adapted from *Daughter of Destiny*
by Jamie Buckingham

On May 9, 1907, sixty miles south of Kansas City in Concordia, Missouri, Joseph and Emma Kuhlman celebrated the birth of their third child, future evangelist, Kathryn Kuhlman. The 160-acre Kuhlman farm was five miles south of Concordia, in Johnson County. Joseph and Emma had moved there immediately after their marriage. The Kuhlmans had two other children, Myrtle the oldest, and Earl their only son.

Kathryn was only six years old when her older sister, Myrtle, married a young student evangelist, Everett B. Parrott, and moved to Chicago. That was three years before Emma gave birth to the last of the Kuhlman children, Geneva. But during that interim, Kathryn and her brother managed to twist their father around their fingers. Papa gave them everything they desired—and left the discipline to Mama.

Kathryn idolized her father. He would sit quietly while she teased his curly hair or ran a comb through his bushy mustache. Often, even after she was a long-legged teenager, he would hold her in his lap and let her lean her head against his shoulder.

In an interview with Jamie Buckingham for her biography, *Daughter of Destiny*, Kathryn said about her parents: "Papa lived and died never having punished me once. He never laid hands on me.... Mama was the one who disciplined me. I got it down in the basement so the neighbors could not hear me scream. Then when Papa came home I would run to him, sit on his lap, and he would take away all the pain.... Mama was the perfect disciplinarian. But she never told me she was proud of me or that I did well. Never once. It was Papa who gave me the love and affection."

In 1921, when Kathryn was fourteen years old, Reverend Hummel, a Baptist evangelist came to Concordia for a two-week revival meeting. The meetings took place at the small Methodist church Emma Kuhlman attended. Kathryn had gone to every meeting that week with her mother, but this day was different. At the close of the Sunday morning service, as the minister gave the invitation, Kathryn began to cry. It wasn't until years later when she evaluated through the filters of experience and time that she comprehended the touch of the Holy Spirit.

Kathryn shook with each sob of her broken heart. Emma looked over at her tall, gangly, fourteen-year-old daughter, but felt helpless to give any kind of encouragement. Like so many in her church, Emma's relationship with God had been a social one, limited to bake sales, missionary society meetings, afternoon teas, and church meetings.

But after her conversion, Kathryn *knew* she was different, life was different; it had taken on a new dimension. She knew that God had something grand in store for her.

Secondary school in Concordia ended with the tenth grade. In 1923, at age sixteen, Kathryn had all the formal education available unless she entered the Lutheran academy. Myrtle, Kathryn's older sister, asked Mama to let Kathryn join her and her husband, Everett, for a series of tent meetings in the northwest. They would keep Kathryn for the summer and then return her in the fall.

Myrtle and Everett Parrott had an evangelistic circuit. They traveled from one town to another, mostly in the Midwest, holding tent revivals. Occasionally Myrtle preached, but most of the time she acted as her husband's business manager.

Emma and Joe didn't want Kathryn to go with the Parrotts, but Myrtle begged her mother, "Mama she must go. I know God wants it. Do you want to stand in God's way?"

After much deliberation the Kuhlmans decided, reluctantly, to let Kathryn go. They suspected, however, that if Kathryn left, she would never return. They were right.

While traveling with Myrtle and Everett, Kathryn helped with the household chores and, as she got accustomed to them, helped with the services as well. Myrtle, who was not happily married, needed Kathryn's joyful presence, and Kathryn needed the stern maturity, yet sisterly kindness, Myrtle provided. The arrangement worked well.

During the evenings, Kathryn attended the revival services with Myrtle—her initiation to tent preaching. Everett Parrott had but one message: "Repent and be saved." He was a shouter. A pulpit thumper. He preached his one message over and over using a variety of texts. By the end of the summer, Kathryn had heard all his sermons several times and was beginning to understand why Myrtle was reluctant to attend the services, even though her husband insisted, often angrily, that he needed her there to help take up the offering and play the piano.

On occasion Kathryn and Myrtle would sing or play a piano duet during the meetings. Twice that summer Parrott asked the sixteen year-old red head to come to the platform and give a testimony, which consisted of her story of conversion in the little Methodist church in Concordia. Both times, she closed the testimony by reciting a lengthy poem, complete with dramatic gestures. The people responded heartily. They loved her drama and the way she pronounced her words. Parrott concluded that if he didn't restrain Kathryn, she could become to him what David was to Saul. Yet, he also knew that if he let Kathryn help take up the offering immediately after she spoke, the people gave more generously.

At the end of the summer, Papa sent money for Kathryn's return trip. With the ticket purchased and everything packed Kathryn began to cry. She realized that she didn't want to leave the ministry, even with its flaws. Myrtle and Everett assured Kathryn that she could stay with them as long as she wished.

Kathryn stayed with Myrtle and Everett for five years. During this time the Parrotts enlisted the services of an extraordinary pianist, Helen Guilliford. Although Helen was eleven years older than Kathryn, they became fast friends.

Financially the ministry looked dismal. Myrtle, Kathryn, and Helen had traveled to Boise, Idaho, where Myrtle preached at services held in the Woman's Club. The offerings were so low that they couldn't make their expenses for renting the building. Since Parrott controlled the funds, Myrtle's only hope was to join Parrott in South Dakota. Both Helen and Kathryn were tired of a fruitless ministry that seemed more riveted with problems than promise. So, when a Nazarene pastor approached them outside the Woman's Club, begging them to stay and preach to the people, Helen and Kathryn agreed to stay.

Kathryn's first sermon on her own was in a dirty little mission church, which used to be a pool hall in a run-down section of Boise. A few old chairs had been pulled in and the piano, which belonged to the boy next door, had been wheeled through the back door. It occupied a place near the rickety pulpit in the corner of the room.

Myrtle shook her head as she left, hoping that her extravagant sister could make it. And make it she did. The people couldn't get enough of her. Kathryn and Helen traveled all over Idaho, spending weeks at a time preaching to a full audience. They billed themselves as "God's Girls." Kathryn once said, "Even then, I knew what God could do if only the gospel—in its simplicity—were preached."

In Joliet, Illinois, Kathryn and Helen spent three months holding services in the second floor of an old store building. While in Joliet, the Evangelical Church Alliance persuaded the young evangelist she needed to be ordained. She agreed, and received the only authorization from the established church she ever had.

One night after the crowd of several hundred left and only a few remained kneeling at the altar in prayer, Kathryn had her first experience with speaking in tongues. Kathryn was sitting with the mother of Isabel Drake, a teacher in Chicago. Isabel knelt at the altar, sometimes sobbing, sometimes praying. Suddenly Isabel rose to a full kneeling position, lifted her face toward the ceiling, and began to sing. Kathryn said, "I had never heard such music. It was the most beautiful singing with the most beautiful voice I had ever heard. She was singing in a language I had never heard, but it was so ethereal, so beautiful, that I felt the hair on my skin rise."

Isabel had never heard of the "gift of tongues," nor had she dreamed that her praying would lead her into this dimension of the Spirit. All she had been doing was asking God to fill her with more of himself.

Events such as this caused Kathryn to dig deep into God's Word, searching for more about the Holy Spirit. Kathryn didn't have formal schooling in theology, but what she did have was an insatiable hunger for God's

Word. "I got my schooling at the feet of the greatest teacher in the world," she later said. "It wasn't in some great university or theological seminary. It was in the school of prayer under the teaching of the Holy Spirit."

Everything Kathryn did was big. When she preached, even if there were only a handful of people in the building, she preached like there were ten thousand. She never let up. At the invitation, she assumed everyone in the congregation needed to repent and give their lives to Christ. Her critics complained when she gushed over some Hollywood movie star or famous political personality. But she also gushed over an obscure priest who had taken a vow of poverty, or over a highway construction worker who had been healed in one of her meetings. She treated taxi drivers and senators just alike—both were equally important in God's eyes, and therefore in hers also.

"Think big. Act big. Talk big," She told her associates. "For we have a big God." In 1933, Kathryn used this principle as she set up her ministry in Denver. This was depression time. Many of the banks across the nation had closed. Every city had breadlines. Unemployment was at its peak. Hundreds of thousands of businesses had closed; and the business that seemed to suffer most was God's business—the Church. Kathryn, who wasn't even a part of the institutional church, but out on the fringes ministering to those who had been rejected by both society and the church, had to be content with whatever financial dregs were available. Nothing seemed to daunt her spirit, however, or cause her to believe in anything less than a God of abundant plenty.

"You go up there to Denver like you've got a million dollars," she told Earl Hewitt, her business manager. "We're going to take that city by storm."

Hewitt gave Kathryn a crooked smile, "But we don't have a million dollars. We have only five dollars. That's all."

Kathryn just laughed. "If we serve a God who is limited to our finances, then we're serving the wrong God. He's not limited to what we have or who we are. If He can use somebody like me to bring souls into the kingdom, He can certainly use our five dollars and multiply it just as easily as He multiplied the loaves and fishes for the people on the hillside. Now go on up to Denver.... This is God's business and we're going to do it God's way. Big."

Kathryn did not reflect the depression. She reflected the greatness of God. Instead of talking lack, she talked plenty. Instead of talking about empty pockets and empty stomachs, she encouraged the people to come and feast at the marriage supper of the Lamb. And the miraculous happened. The people brought their loaves and fishes, their small offerings, and they were multiplied a thousand-fold. Instead of sending the people to degrading soup lines run by the state and federal governments, she encouraged those who had food to bring it and share it with those who had none.

There were only 125 people present the first night of their campaign (August 27, 1933), but she preached as though there were 12,000. The following night there were 400 people, and from then on the old warehouse could not hold the crowds.

After five months of continuous services, Kathryn was ready to move on. She had remained in Denver longer than any other place she'd preached since she had begun her ministry. When she announced her intention to leave, the crowds protested.

One member in the crowd promised to personally finance the down payment on the biggest building she could find if she promised to stay. A search began for a place to build the tabernacle. In the meantime Kathryn moved the meeting place of the church to the empty warehouse of the Monitor Paper Company at 1941 Curtis Street. They placed a sign outside the building naming it the KUHLMAN REVIVAL TABERNACLE.

Helen Gulliford formed a choir of over one hundred voices and composed much of the music they sang. Outside speakers were brought in to teach and feed the people of the fastest growing assembly in the West.

It was in the paper warehouse that Kathryn began to be exposed to the concepts of divine healing. Healing services were often held at the close of the evangelistic meetings, and the guest preacher would ask all the sick to come forward for special prayer. On some occasions they would be anointed with oil. On other occasions they would be asked to go to a back room for special prayer. Kathryn, although she seldom prayed for the sick herself, was always amazed and gratified when people were healed.

In early 1935, the group of men who were searching for a permanent home for Kathryn's ministry found an ideal spot for a tabernacle. It was an old truck garage, formerly the livery stable for the Daniel and Fisher department store. Renovation work began on February 5th and four months later, on May 30th, the huge building, complete with 2,000 seats was filled to overflowing for the dedication service. A seventy-two foot neon sign running the length of the building, said: "DENVER REVIVAL TABERNACLE."

The services remained the same. Helen played the piano and then during the altar calls roamed up and down the aisles looking for people who held up their hands for prayer and inviting them to the front. Kathryn preached. At the close of each service—from 10:00 until 10:15—Kathryn went on the air, live, over KVOD radio for her program, "Smiling Through."

It was here at the Denver Revival Tabernacle that Kathryn's mama came to know Christ, one night after an evangelistic service. After receiving the anointing of the Holy Spirit, Emma reached out for her daughter and held her tightly. It was the first time that Kathryn could ever remember being embraced by her mother. "Kathryn, preach that others might receive what I have just received," Mama wept. "Preach and don't ever stop."

Work on the Denver Revival Tabernacle was never really completed. The brick walls, the heating plant, the wiring and the plumbing—all needed constant care. During the week the men who were without jobs would show up at the tabernacle in work parties. The women, with Kathryn and Helen leading the way, brought in food. The men, who didn't have money to buy food of their own, carried home what was left over each day.

In 1937 a handsome evangelist from Austin, Texas, Burroughs A. Waltrip came to preach at the tabernacle. He had been recommended by Phil Kerr, the radio evangelist. His preaching and demeanor thrilled Kathryn. At thirty-eight, he was eight years older than Kathryn. She later described him as "the best-looking guy that ever was." Good looks and good preaching made a good combination, and Kathryn invited him back in the fall of the year.

This time his wife, Jessie, and their two sons, aged six and eight, came along. There was some speculation at the time that Jessie was uncomfortable with her rangy, dark-haired, husband spending too much time with the long-legged redhead. She wanted to be around to keep an eye on him—and them. The people in Denver found Jessie Waltrip to be quiet and unassuming, an ideal wife for the dynamic preacher.

But something happened during Waltrip's second visit to Denver. The facts are unclear. Mrs. Waltrip took the boys and returned to Austin. It was time to enter them in school. A month later Waltrip wrote his wife saying he was not coming home. The report he gave in Denver, however, was that Jessie had deserted him. He had pled, he said, for her to join him, but she refused. Charging her with desertion, he traveled north to Mason City, Iowa, near the Minnesota border. The people in Mason City were impressed with his preaching. They encouraged him to stay and begin a work similar to that which Kathryn had in Denver. It wasn't long before Waltrip had obtained a big building, which he renovated and called THE RADIO CHAPEL—since he was also using it for daily broadcasts over KGLO.

Kathryn helped Waltrip raise funds for his Radio Chapel by holding preaching services in Mason City. When Kathryn returned to Denver she and Burroughs had made plans for their marriage—his divorce was final. Helen Gulliford had seen it coming for a long time.

"She was beginning to feel that life was passing her by," Helen told a close friend. She could see that Kathryn was changing. Her preaching, once so dynamic, was becoming weak. Helen lamented, as God left Kathryn to her own devices. She was strong enough and had enough personal magnetism to make it on her own, to fool some of the people all the time. But the more discerning members of the congregation began to realize that their Kathryn was not the same. Headstrong, she was determined to have her own way—even if it meant the destruction of her entire ministry.

Only two people from the Denver Revival Tabernacle attended the wedding—Ina Fooks and Earl Hewitt. Before the service Hewitt met with Kathryn and explained the situation. Helen Gulliford had resigned from the Kuhlman ministry. She would stay in Denver to work with one of the groups that had already pulled away from the tabernacle. Hewitt said Kathryn would never again be welcome in Denver. He offered to buy her share of the building. She accepted and handed him the keys to her kingdom.

Halfway through the wedding ceremony she fainted. Waltrip helped revive her. Clutching her arm, he guided her through the remaining vows. For the next six years, Kathryn wandered backslidden and virtually useless to the ministry of God.

Nobody knows exactly when Waltrip and Kathryn separated, but it probably was in 1944. She said she had to make a choice. "Would I serve the man I loved, or the God I loved. I knew I could not serve God and live with Mister." She called Waltrip "Mister" from the very first time she met him. "No one will ever know the pain of dying like I know it, for I loved him more than I loved life itself. And for a time, I loved him even more than God. I finally told him I had to leave. God had never released me from that original call. Not only did I live with [Mister], I had to live with my conscience, and the conviction of the Holy Spirit was almost unbearable. I was tired of trying to justify myself."

After Kathryn separated from Waltrip she went to Franklin, Pennsylvania, a town of about 10,000 in the northwest sector of the state between Pittsburgh and Erie. She called Matthew J. Maloney who owned the Gospel Tabernacle. He had been impressed with Kathryn when she visited Franklin previously. The old tabernacle seated 1,500 and was filled from the very beginning. Encouraged by her reception, Kathryn started to branch out. Radio was the natural medium.

In the spring of 1946, Kathryn asked a few relevant questions, insisted on a certain time every morning, and procured a time slot from radio station WKRZ in nearby Oil City. She left without ever inquiring about the cost. If God had told her to broadcast and had given her the time, she'd let Him worry about the cost. It was a procedure she would follow the rest of her life.

By midsummer, Kathryn's fame had spread and so had her ministry. She added a radio station in Pittsburgh, which broadcast the programs originating in Oil City. But her popularity brought its own set of problems. Her loyal followers wanted to get close to her, but were unable to at the tabernacle meetings, so they came to the radio station instead. They would sit in the lobby and watch Kathryn through the large glass window. Soon the lobby was so packed with people the station personnel could not do their work. When some of the people began to react emotionally, even hysterically, crying out to God in confession or weeping as they fell under conviction, the radio station had to bar all visitors from the studio. The people, hungry to be fed from the Word of God, flocked to her work and her ministry blossomed, increasing in breadth, followers, and impact.

She continued to reach people where they were through her evangelistic services, radio programs, and eventually through television. God chose Kathryn Kuhlman as His handmaiden to touch hundreds of thousands of lives through preaching and prayer and to bring healing to His people. She was not perfect, she never claimed to be, but she was willing. She died on February 20, 1976, a faithful servant to the God she loved.

Twenty-five years have passed since her death, but her ministry lives on through the recordings and messages she left behind. The warm style that personified

Kathryn Kuhlman shines through this transcription of her Beatitudes sermons, which were originally recorded during the 1950s at her Pittsburgh radio station.

Kathryn, 3 months old

Kuhlman Family Portrait: (left to right) brother Earl;
father Joe Kuhlman; mother Emma; Kathryn; sister Myrtle

Home in Concordia, Missouri where Kathryn lived and
Papa was mayor

Kathryn Kuhlman as a child

Mrs. Joe Kuhlman
(holding Geneva),
Myrtle and Kathryn

Kathryn Kuhlman
as a child

18

Times of relaxing for the young "preacher"

Kathryn. The sense of humor so many enjoyed

Kathryn with Helen Gulliford, her pianist

Kathryn, "just arrived"

The "preacher" on the back steps of the church

Denver Revival Tabernacle

Kathryn outside Tabernacle

Kathryn at the Tabernacle ground-breaking

Prayer meeting night at the Denver Tabernacle

Kathryn and Eve Conley

Sunday parking at Faith Temple at Sugar Creek, PA

With her basket in which Kathryn carried her Bible

On the grounds at Faith Temple

*One of the first radio stations to air the
Kathryn Kuhlman program*

A service at Faith Temple

*Carnegie Auditorium,
first Pittsburgh "home"
of miracle services
which began in 1948.*

Kathryn's radio studio in Carlton House in Pittsburgh

Kathryn with her concert choir in Pittsburgh

*Food for the needy, one of the charitable activities
Kathryn sponsored*

Autographing her first book, I Believe in Miracles, *which is a multimillion-copy best-seller*

First nation-wide publicity in Redbook Magazine, *1950*

Maggie Hartner, Kathryn and Eve Conley

Fifth Anniversary in Pittsburgh,
celebrated at Syria Mosque, 1953

*Christmas party for 500 youngsters from Children's Church
at Stambaugh Auditorium, Youngstown, Ohio*

Baptismal service at Brady's Run Park, 1958

Twenty-five years in Pittsburgh, with Maggie Hartner

The Beatitudes

A nd seeing the multitudes, Jesus went up into a mountain: and when he was set, his disciples came unto him:

And he opened his mouth, and taught them, saying,

Blessed are the poor in spirit: for theirs is the kingdom of heaven.

Blessed are they that mourn: for they shall be comforted.

Blessed are the meek: for they shall inherit the earth.

Blessed are they which do hunger and thirst after righteousness: for they shall be filled.

Blessed are the merciful: for they shall obtain mercy.

Blessed are the pure in heart: for they shall see God.

Blessed are the peacemakers: for they shall be called the children of God.

Blessed are they which are persecuted for righteousness' sake: for theirs is the kingdom of heaven.

Blessed are ye, when men shall revile you, and persecute you, and shall say all manner of evil against you falsely, for my sake.

Rejoice, and be exceeding glad: for great is your reward in heaven: for so persecuted they the prophets which were before you.

Ye are the salt of the earth: but if the salt have lost his savor, wherewith shall it be salted? It is thenceforth good for nothing, but to be cast out, and to be trodden under foot of men.

Ye are the light of the world. A city that is set on a hill cannot be hid.

Neither do men light a candle, and put it under a bushel, but on a candlestick; and it giveth light unto all that are in the house.

Let your light so shine before men, that they may see your good works, and glorify your Father which is in heaven.

Matthew 5:1-16

ONE

Poor in Spirit

As we begin this study, let us pause to picture Jesus sitting there on the side of the mountain surrounded by His disciples and the multitudes who had followed Him. If you have travelled to the Holy Land, perhaps you have walked over the same ground where those people gathered. As I made my way over portions of Israel, I have wondered if I was standing on the soil where Jesus stood. I may have climbed the same hill. Perhaps I saw the very spot where Jesus sat down and said, "Blessed arc the poor in spirit."

Have you ever wondered if those who were listening to Him really understood? Or have you questioned if you or I would have comprehended the real depth of meaning of His words if we had been there? To my thinking, and living as we do in this materialistic world, the very minute the word "poor" left Jesus' lips, the masses immediately equated "poor" with a lack of money; but the possession of money alone does not make a person rich. One's wealth cannot always be measured by material gains or accumulations;

and the word *rich* can have a meaning quite different from mere material possessions. One can be rich in the things of God, or rich in mind, rich in heart, rich in spirit, and still possess little material wealth.

Now when Jesus said, "Blessed are the poor in spirit," I am sure there were some in the gathering who lost interest immediately. But do you want to know what the word "poor" means here? One must become poor—poor in a deep sense of nothingness before God—to truly be rich in the things of God. I will admit that is a most difficult hurdle and one of the hardest achievements for any man. We are part of a generation whose doctrine is self-sufficiency, which is absolutely contrary to the teaching of the Lord Jesus Christ. The very things that Jesus was preaching in this sermon were contrary to their theology then, and modern theology now; contrary to man's thinking then, and man's thinking now. Man's doctrine, man's theology, man's rules for living are, in a sense, a code of self-sufficiency; and that is why it is very difficult for man to get to the place where he can come into the presence of Almighty God and actually have a feeling of complete nothingness, where he can be absolutely resigned before the giving hand of his Lord. The foundation of all spiritual happiness is a consciousness before God of one's emptiness and one's need.

Jesus tells us in this first beatitude—poverty of spirit—that we must be aware of our lack of God. When we get to that place (and it is not easy, believe me), we have laid the foundation for genuine wealth. You and I will never inherit the Kingdom of Heaven until we get to the place where we acknowledge our absolute nothingness. Real riches come from God. Real blessings come from the giver of every good and perfect gift. Real wealth cannot be bought with dollars and cents, for we cannot purchase even the smallest blessing from God.

If you want to be truly rich, you must come to the place where you have a deep sense of nothingness before God; and that, my friend, is what Jesus meant when He said, "Blessed are the poor in spirit." The realization of our lack of God is the poverty that makes rich. And when you come to the place where you can face yourself, face God, and realize your lack of Him and your need of Him—when you get to the place where you recognize your nothingness, it is then that you are on the road to becoming rich.

But Jesus does not stop there. He continues by saying, "Theirs *is* the kingdom of Heaven." He is telling us that we have immediate possession of the Kingdom of Heaven *now*! We don't need to die to be a part of the Kingdom of Heaven, but sometimes we have such false ideas. We are so farsighted—looking for the glories of the Kingdom after death. That is not God's plan. You and I can be rich now! We can inherit and be a part of the Kingdom of Heaven now! Our only limitation is our capability of receiving what Jesus promised us.

Please turn with me to another portion of Scripture, a verse which is familiar to all of us: "Suffer the little children to come unto me, and forbid them not: for of such is the kingdom of God" (Mark 10:14).

The Kingdom of God belongs to the little children in exactly the same way the Kingdom of Heaven belongs to the poor in spirit. Its powers are theirs. You see, the poor in spirit, those who acknowledge their absolute nothingness in God's presence, can be likened to a little child: simple, unaffected, and teachable. It is when we possess the spirit like that of a little child that we are able to realize our nothingness and come to the knowledge that all our sufficiency is of God. Only then can we inherit His Kingdom. These two classes—the poor in spirit and those who possess the spirit of a little child—are one and the same in God's sight; and right here we find the key that unlocks the resources of the storehouse of the universe, and the wealth of it all is ours.

There is a parallel to the Christian concept of entire surrender to the will of God that I have found most interesting. It is what science seems to teach in most unmistakable terms. Let me explain what I mean. Science says: sit down before the facts as a little child. Be prepared to give up every preconceived notion, every preconceived idea. Be willing to follow to whatever end nature will lead you, or you will know nothing.

How does a scientist gain mastery over nature? There is only one way: by surrendering to it. If the scientist is proud and unteachable, he will learn nothing. He will master nothing. Every great scientist is a humble man. I have listened to them and I am amazed at their humility, awed by their absolute unpretentiousness. I am of the true belief that every really great scientist is a humble person. He advances, as it were, upon his knees. Then, he stands straight and masterful, and all the powers of nature are at his disposal. The meek, the Word of God says, inherit the earth; so you, too, inherit its powers as you surrender to the Kingdom of Heaven.

As we look further into this study of the poor in spirit, some will immediately feel they have nothing to learn from it, for their status already is poverty. But I am not talking about the kind of poverty that concerns one's bank account. I have known people who are proud of their poverty. They glory in it, just as some people have too much fun being sick to ever be well physically. They can talk about their sicknesses, and enjoy the sympathy they receive; and sometimes I wonder whether there is really much wrong with them. But, you see, it makes them the center of attention, and if ever they were perfectly well, they would lose their crutch. No, I am not talking about that kind of poverty. I am talking about being poor in spirit, a poverty which can bring one the greatest accumulation of wealth that a human being can know.

Let me direct your attention to a book in the Old Testament, the thirteenth chapter of Numbers. Twelve men were sent to spy out the Promised Land. Ten of them returned and gave a disheartening report. They said, "And there we saw the giants … and we were in our own sight as grasshoppers." But two of them saw victory through the eyes of God for they said, "Let us go up at once, and possess it; for we are well able to overcome it" (Numbers 13:30).

In Matthew 25:14-30, we read of the servants to whom were entrusted talents. The man with one talent was poor and do you know why? Because he buried his talent in the ground. There are a lot of people who lack the courage to use the talents that are theirs. They are poor, indeed. On the other hand, there is the other extreme: an overabundance of self-confidence, which is a form of poverty also. I believe Peter typified that type of poverty when he boastfully said, "Though all men shall be offended because of thee, yet will I never be offended" (Matthew 26:33). At this period in Peter's life, he was boastful and had yet to learn to be poor in spirit.

In Luke 18:10-14 we read of two men who went up to the temple to pray. One said, "God, I thank thee, that I am not as other men are." He was very satisfied with himself and I do not believe God heard one word of his prayer. I can picture that old fellow standing where everybody would be sure to see him pray. They may have considered him a very spiritual person, and thought, "What a good man. Look how sincere he is!" But that which was in his heart and mind became evident when he said, "God, I thank thee, that I am not as other men are." You know, one can criticize another only after he has become satisfied with himself. In this case, this man's spiritual vision was distorted and warped as he focused on his neighbors' shortcomings, and on his own good qualities. There are some of us, too, who could use a change of spiritual glasses because our own spiritual sight is not clear. We need to see ourselves as God and others see us.

But let us notice now the publican who "smote upon his breast, saying, God be merciful to me a sinner." He did not look upon his neighbor, but saw his own sins. That man may have possessed great material wealth. He may have had the courage of a mighty conqueror; but he realized that he lacked something that God alone could supply. Thus, the poverty which is a key to God's kingdom, is the realization that even though we may possess all things, all things are nothing without God.

If you can get to the place where you can realize that all things are nothing without God—no matter what you have, though you may possess all that this world counts as riches—then you have learned the secret of being numbered among the poor in spirit, those who possess all things through Jesus Christ.

God's Kingdom becomes an immediate possession when we become joint-heirs with Jesus Christ. Remember: God's Kingdom is not a place. It is not an experience. It is not bounded by geographical lines. It is bounded only by our capacity to receive it. It can be likened to sanctification, and we do not seek sanctification. We seek Jesus, and only when we have Jesus and have surrendered everything to Him will we be sanctified. Neither do we seek the Kingdom of Heaven, but it is bounded by our capacity to receive it. When we have met the conditions and we have come on God's terms, having paid the price of complete surrender, we will know that we have entered into the Kingdom of Heaven. In possessing the Kingdom, we possess all things.

I beg you—keep your eyes on Jesus. With your eyes on Him you will not seesaw in your emotions. You will not be rich one moment and poverty-stricken the next. God is the same when the paycheck is coming in and when it fails. Listen to the words God spoke to Joshua and all Israel following Moses' death: "Be strong and of a good courage; be not afraid, neither be thou dismayed: for the Lord thy God is with thee whithersoever thou goest" (Joshua 1:9).

The journey of the children of Israel through the wilderness is an example to us here and now. They had placed their faith in Moses. Then he died and they were terrified. He had been their leader, their crutch, their strength, and their courage. They had leaned on him for everything. But God had everything under control!

Do you want to know Joshua's secret for courage? He belonged to the kingdom of God. Joshua was wearing the right kind of glasses and he was looking in the right direction. He was a spiritual giant because he knew in whom he had placed his faith; thus he could heed God's words: "BE STRONG!" He was not rich one moment and poverty-stricken the next. He was rich under ALL circumstances. Had Joshua not possessed courage himself—had he not been strong spiritually within, he could not have instilled confidence and assurance in the hearts of the children of Israel.

Joshua is the perfect example today of what it means to belong to the Kingdom of Heaven. Possessing God's power enables us to face life with enthusiasm. It gives us a deep inward peace because we are not afraid of tomorrow, and there comes into our lives an inner joy that outward circumstances can never touch, because

God is within us and God is love. As a result, there flows out from us a love for others that sweeps aside all prejudice, all jealousy, and all hatred.

The Kingdom of Heaven is about belonging! First of all, we belong to Jesus and that is the greatest joy in the world. Do you want to know what really gives me joy and happiness? It's not something external. Sometimes I wish I could get more enthusiastic about things that are external, and I wish I could recapture some of the emotions I had when I was a little girl. But my real happiness and my real joy come from within, from knowing that I belong to God, that He is my heavenly Father, and that I am a part of His kingdom. I face every day with that glorious knowledge. It gives me a deep inward peace and removes all fear for tomorrow. Why should I be afraid of what tomorrow will bring when I am an heir of God and a joint-heir with Christ Jesus? I am a part of His Kingdom and in the light of these blessings, all other possessions are empty and grow dim and fall short of His glory. Therefore, I look up and thank God that I became poor in spirit; in return, He gives to me day after day the joy and assurance of having a part in the Kingdom of Heaven.

TWO

They That Mourn

" **B**lessed are they that mourn: for they shall be comforted." Mourning is not something for which we strive in life. To the natural mind, it is as undesirable as poverty, but only those who can feel can really mourn.

Our Lord said, "Blessed are they that mourn." He was not referring to the pessimist, nor to the selfish person whose ambitions are foremost in his thinking, neither did He have in mind the person bitter over some loss. There are men and women whose tears can flow as easily as water spouting from an open faucet. But long ago I learned that there are different kinds of tears. Some are shed because of jealousy. I'm sure you are aware that the first weapon a jealous person will use is tears. In situations like that, I find I have to check myself for it is my first impulse to confront them with the fact that I know their crying is only a sham and a weapon to gain their own way.

Then there are tears of self-pity. Those are the people who have lived a lifetime of feeling sorry for themselves and have worked hard to gain sympathy on every side.

Yes, I have found that nothing can mean so little as tears, and nothing can mean so much as tears. I have dealt with men who were scarred and hardened by the cares of life. They have knelt with me and I have prayed with them; yet, I was aware that I was not getting through to the heart and into their soul. Then, suddenly, as I was about to give up, I saw one falling tear or a glistening in an eye. In that instant I knew that a softening process was beginning to take place, and that the Holy Spirit had pierced through the tough exterior and was reaching into the heart.

If you have no sensitivity whatsoever when it comes to spiritual things (perhaps you are even boastful of this fact), if you can honestly say your emotions are not stirred when you read the Bible, if you admit that you have no conscience concerning the things of God, then I pray you will take stock of your soul now before another hour passes.

Too many people today desire God's blessings, but not the cleansing and purifying discipline of His Word. Scores seek and accept sermons that tickle the ears, but remember: Christ came to create a new heart in mankind rather than treat the symptoms of their dilemmas alone. Yes, the feeling that many want as a result of their religion is a good feeling—one of security. They look for a preacher to pat them on the back and tell them that they are really not so bad after all. But Christ did not come to make us satisfied with the life that we are now living. Jesus never preached a sermon without pointing His finger directly into the face of those that were listening. He called sin, SIN.

There is another scripture that I want to share in connection with this subject, so turn now to the Gospel of Mark where we read that James and John came to Jesus with a special request. I have wondered if these two brothers were a part of the vast congregation that sat on the mountainside when Jesus preached His great sermon that we call "The Beatitudes." If these sons of Zebedee were there, I have a feeling that they missed His point entirely as so many of us do today.

"And James and John, the sons of Zebedee, come unto Him, saying, Master, we would that thou shouldest do for us whatsoever we shall desire" (Mark 10:35). In other words they had a favor to ask of Jesus. Jesus said, "What would ye that I should do for you?" And this was their request: "Grant unto us that we may sit, one on thy right hand, and the other on thy left hand, in thy glory." They wanted to be seated on either side of Jesus. But Jesus replied that He had no seats to give. It was not in His power to give seats. To follow in His footsteps did not insure a seat, but a cup. Not a seat but a cross. (See Mark 10:35-40.)

It has been my observation that spectators are never healthy or victorious Christians. Too many who are professing Christ as Savior exercise their Christianity passively, like someone watching a movie or viewing a television screen. Their thrill and adventure come to them second-hand. They wish to receive everything while seated, without doing a thing, without paying a price. But you and I cannot understand or realize true Christianity from a seat, and neither will we become deeply spiritual from a seat. The cup the Master offers is sometimes filled with sorrow or tribulation or bitter waters. Yes, we are assured of and long for God's blessings. We yearn to experience the glories of heaven and desire heaven's best, but without the pain of God's purging.

There are many who will argue: "I am caught in a web of circumstance that binds me hand and foot. How can I live the abundant life? How can I be victorious? No one understands my situation. Surely, I am an exception when it comes to winning the battle and finding comfort through the power of the Holy Spirit."

In answer, let me refer you to a passage of Scripture in Jeremiah 31:2, which refers to the children of Israel as they left Egypt for the Promised Land: "Thus saith the LORD, The people which were left of the sword found grace in the wilderness." These people were purified in their exile, and they became instruments of God through that terrible experience of national wandering. The wilderness—though grievous and despised—became a door to victory for them.

God's grace is very often found in our wilderness experiences or in our dungeons. It is possible for you to find it in your Gethsemane hour and in your suffering. You may gain no release from the dungeon that has imprisoned you, but you can obtain grace that gives you victory while in that dungeon. Your Gethsemane need not be a tragedy. Through God it can become the greatest experience of your life. Therefore, do not wallow in your suffering but accept your circumstance as a challenge. Consider your trial to be an opportunity for God to work in and through you, and to cause you to be creative.

We put much stress on having a well and healthy body; and it is also vitally important to have a well and healthy mind. Yet, there is something that is far more important than physical and mental health; and that is a healthy soul and spiritual life. When we receive spiritual healing of the soul, frustrations must go and in their place we find usefulness and an outgoing love. Every day will be a challenge. We give of ourselves and ask nothing in return. Self is forgotten.

Among the greatest spiritual giants who ever lived was the Apostle Paul. We cannot fully appreciate his spiritual strength until we take time to study the characteristics of his life. In his letters, written while in prison, we see a man of great strength and depth. There was no hint of self-pity although he was imprisoned. He wrote from his cell without thought of himself because he had found glorious power in the mighty Comforter. He had found grace sufficient for all his needs and grace enough to spare.

Over and over again I have made this statement but I'll make it again: *you can never give to anyone else any more than you have experienced yourself.* We must experience to truly live. We must pass through the deep waters to become a mature person. We reach maturity as a Christian only as we gain victory over each hurdle. Finally, every crisis becomes a challenge, an adventure, and an opportunity to put God's promises to the test.

Do you want to know the reality of the promises of God? You will never experience this joy from a seat. You will never experience His faithfulness from a spectator's position. Only as you personally stand at the very edge of your Red Sea, where you cannot go forward and there is no way back, will you discover the certainty of God's unchanging Word. You can choose to go down in defeat, or you can turn to the Word of God, stake your very life on His promises that cannot lie, and be victorious.

You may receive deep spiritual teaching under the leadership of a true man of God and hold membership in his congregation, but you will never know the reality of the living Word of God until you rely on God's promises for yourself and put His Word to the test. And you will never put God's Word to the test until you become desperate and stand at the brink of your Red Sea where God is your last hope. Then, in desperation, you dare to believe His Word and stand firmly upon "thus saith the Lord."

Do you want to know the tenderness of the Man of Sorrows? Then, my friend, go to your Gethsemane. Look up when the night is dark and the very stars in the heavens have ceased to shine upon your life. In that moment you will become conscious of the presence of One who can be more real than any human being you have ever known. You will feel a tenderness in the person of Jesus. You will sense the Master's strong arms holding you close to His great heart.

"For they shall be comforted." The word *comforted* has a meaning different from sympathy. In Jesus' presence, you will find comfort but not sympathy. He gives sympathy to no man, and His gift to His church, the Holy Spirit, gives sympathy to no person. But you can be sure that the mighty Comforter will give you His comfort! He will give you power! He will give you strength! He will impart His courage to you, and you will find yourself doing that which you could not do in your own strength or under your own power.

Blessed are they that mourn, blessed are they who go through Gethsemane, for it is there that they grow. You and I will never be spiritual giants or mature spiritually, we will never know the tenderness of the Man of Sorrows if we allow bitterness to enter our hearts and our minds. If we suffer, we shall also reign with Him. There is a crown of glory, there is a reward awaiting those of us who suffer for His Name's sake and come through that suffering victoriously—not in our own strength, but in the strength of the mighty Comforter, the Holy Spirit.

Yes, we desire God's blessing, but we shrink from the pain of His purging. Yet, my friend, we can never know that cherished nearness or the glories of heaven's best without the painful purging; and we have God's promise that with the pain and the purging will come the strengthening power of the Holy Ghost, the mighty Comforter of the Trinity. Jesus said, I cannot give you seats, but I offer you a cup filled with sorrow even as My cup. And a cross: "And whosoever doth not bear his cross, and come after me, cannot be my disciple" (Luke 14:27).

THREE

Blessed Are the Meek

Now we come to the third in the list of Beatitudes: "Blessed are the meek: for they shall inherit the earth." I must admit that not many people earnestly desire to be meek. Be honest with yourself; look yourself directly in the face, and you (like most of us) will have to say, "I do not want to be meek!" We do not seek to acquire the meekness of a lamb, but rather prefer the qualities of a mighty tiger.

Watch something. We all have the tendency to shy away from the word "meekness." We think of meekness as weakness, but Jesus did not use the word here in that sense. No, in His statement He was not speaking of a weakling. Sometimes I think we purposely misunderstand the word "meek" because we are afraid of the demands such a decision will place upon our life—surrender. Meekness represents complete surrender.

To completely surrender oneself to God is one of the most difficult things that a human being can do. Remember the scientist to whom I called your attention in an earlier chapter. It is his meekness that gains him power over nature. The scholar who is meek gains power over knowledge. And the Christian who is meek gains power over the world. Jesus stated this truth in these words: "Blessed are the meek: for they shall inherit the Earth."

Our Lord's words here may seem almost absurd to some. Inherit Heaven? Yes, we can understand that, and we all look forward to the day when we see Jesus and Heaven becomes our home. But inherit the Earth here and now, in this lifetime? You say, "No." But in reality the meek do inherit the Earth, and they are the only ones in whose hands is given power to inherit the Earth.

Let us consider a parallel. To whom do the stars belong? The stars belong to the astronomer who meekly surrenders to them. He enters the kingdom of the stars through that surrender. He is the one who can fully appreciate and enjoy the stars, and he is very conscious of their power.

To whom do the mountains belong? The mountains belong to the geologist who loves them, who surrenders to them, and therefore gains their secrets and is at home with them. He appreciates them for he has yielded himself to them.

Who inherits the world of the mind? Is it those who say that they are free to do as they like with their minds? No! There is literally a place where man can surrender not only his body to Christ, but his mind as well. That one who meekly surrenders his mind to Christ is thus ruled by Christ. It is then that the mind of Christ governs his thinking, that a greater understanding of spiritual things is imparted to him, and he has a greater understanding of the things of this Earth and those things beyond this Earth.

God alone imparts great wisdom, divine wisdom—His wisdom. It is the Christian who surrenders himself and his mind to God, who inherits the world of the mind. Therefore, Jesus was right (as always) for the meek do inherit the Earth.

Over and over again I have been made to realize that no man really learns how to live, and no individual possesses the secret of living, until he surrenders himself—body and soul—to the Lord. The Hebrew word that is translated "meek" really means "to be molded." As you surrender yourself in meekness to Christ, you allow yourself to be as putty in God's hands, to be molded by Him.

Yield yourself to the purposes of God. If you allow your life to be controlled by God, you will discover the greatest possible secret in living. I would be afraid to face the future, and I would be numbered among those engulfed by fear, had I not given myself over to God's control. One cannot deny that fear is one of the most devastating emotions that men and women can take into their lives. But I am not afraid because I have given myself to a power that is greater than myself. I have given myself over to God's control. I have perfect confidence in His power and His ability. I know He will take care of today and tomorrow and all the tomorrows of my life.

Beloved, the word meekness means to be controlled by, to be submissive to, the divine plan of God. Do not forget that the laws of God were already established when we were born. His ways are fixed, but we have a choice in that we can accept God's ways and live according to His laws, or we can rebel against Him and His rules. But we cannot change what He has already done.

If I am not making this point clear to you, let me share here an example given by a Christian gentleman with keen insight. It is fact that the world is round and the sky is blue. If someone says he does not like round worlds or blue skies and would rather have a square world and a green sky, there is nothing that person can do to change what already exists. God's world is round and His sky is blue, and so they shall remain.

God's laws of the universe are as unchangeable as is His universe itself. He has created seasons of the year. The farmer learns the laws of the seasons, and he is governed by them. He plants his crops when they should be planted, and thus he reaps when he should reap. He would get into a heap of trouble if he would rather sow his corn in winter. Why? Because in doing so he is working contrary to God's laws of the universe. A wise farmer cooperates and yields to God's laws. He has learned the laws of the seasons, and he is governed by them. Therefore, he plants his crops when they should be planted and reaps when he should reap. For him to rebel against God's laws and plant out of season does not alter the laws of God. It only produces failure of his own crop and *he* is the loser. Therefore, for the farmer, meekness means planting when he should plant. It means submission to God's laws.

So it is with life. God has His will, and man has his will. Man has his choice of exerting his self-will or submitting to God's will in meekness. You and I can go against God's will or we can submit to the will of God.

We have the greatest example of meekness in the life of Jesus himself. Jesus knew what He was talking about when He said, "Blessed are the meek," for Jesus was man as much as He was God. Therefore, in His humanity, He had a will of His own. Even as He sat on that hillside teaching the very thing that I am giving you now, He knew that He had a will of His own which was a will separate and apart from the will of God the Father. Jesus was preaching about one of the most difficult choices confronting each human being: to surrender to the Father, rather than to elect to do one's own will. Jesus himself found it necessary to submit and surrender His will to the Father's will, for He said, "Nevertheless not my will, but thine, be done" (Luke 22:42).

In Psalm 37:4 we read: "Delight thyself also in the LORD; and he shall give thee the desires of thine heart." In other words, under the inspiration of the Holy Spirit, the Psalmist is saying: When a human being delights himself in the Lord and becomes submissive to the Lord, he yields to a power greater than himself. Then, as a result, the Lord himself gives to that one the desires of his heart.

On the other hand, for one to fail to become molded or controlled by God's will is to miss God's best and to destroy oneself. It is impossible to go against the laws of God, to fight against the will of God, to live a life of rebellion toward God—and experience joy and peace.

One of the greatest things in the world is to have peace of mind. Are you among those wondering why peace of mind and peace of soul always seem to elude your grasp? Pause for a minute to analyze yourself, your purposes, and your situation. Are you fighting against the laws of God and, as a result, lacking the joy of knowing peace? Are you demanding your own will and insisting on having your own way? If your answer is "yes," perhaps you do not like the results. It is possible that your way has played havoc with your life and you are the loser.

If you are such a person, then some place and somewhere along the line you have been fighting against God's laws. If this describes you, then you are like the foolish farmer planting seeds in winter when they should be planted in the spring. You are wanting green skies when God has made them blue. You are wanting a square world when God has made the world round.

Be practical about this thing. You cannot expect peace of mind when everything you do is contrary to the will and the laws of God, and you are working in opposition to God's will and His laws. Under these circumstances, you cannot expect things to go right for you. You are heading down a one-way street, going in the wrong direction. Didn't you see that sign informing you that you were travelling the wrong way? You chose to travel in the wrong direction, but it isn't too late to change! Look up. Take your eyes off yourself long enough to see where the arrow is pointing. Realize that you are moving in a direction opposed to where God's arrow is directing you. All God's laws point in one direction: to himself, but you are living contrary to His will and His purposes.

"Blessed are the meek," Jesus said, and the meek— those who surrender to God—possess God. Those who surrender to Him will have peace. Those who surrender to His will possess joy. "Perfect love casteth out fear" (1 John 4:18), but you must love Him enough to become submissive to Him surrendering all to God, and then you will be numbered among the meek who inherit the earth.

FOUR

They Which Do Hunger and Thirst

Thousands sat on the side of the mountain, and Jesus spoke to them in a language that they could understand, using words such as hunger and thirst; and He said, "Blessed are they which do hunger and thirst after righteousness: for they shall be filled." The hunger and thirst of which He spoke, however, were not physical, but spiritual. He was not referring to a desire easily satisfied by human provisions. He spoke, rather, of a yearning to attain holiness and righteousness, which is complete conformity to the precious will of God.

Sometimes our human appetites are too easily satisfied. Swine, you know, are content with husks; but not the soul of the immortal human. It is the desire for holiness that is blessed of God. It is the desire for the spiritual that is blessed of Him. It is the desire for the deeper things of God that He blesses and rewards.

It is the desire to know Him and a desire for righteousness, and a desire for the knowledge of the Word of God, that the Lord satisfies.

See something here—our hunger and thirst come from our hungering and thirsting souls, but the perfection and satisfaction of these longings remain on God's side to give. He is the giver. We receive holiness, but we do not create it. When the hunger and the thirst for spiritual things is there, He is the one who has promised to give satisfaction in order that the hunger may be appeased, I have learned that it is possible that spiritual hunger can far outweigh any hunger experienced by the physical body.

I have known people who say they are hungry for the things of God, but I have discovered they do not really mean it, because their actions speak contrary to their words. They say "I want to be a Christian but I cannot find Christ." Every time an invitation is given, they are among the first to make their way to the altar. I do not believe it necessary to repeatedly run to an altar to receive Christ. On the authority of God's Word, I promise you that you need come but once. When you want Jesus, when you long for that new-birth experience that He has provided, when you desire more than anything else in the world the assurance that your sins are covered with the blood of Christ, then you will receive that experience, and you will know that God's Son has cleansed you from all sin. But, you must desire Him with all your heart and soul—therein lies the secret.

Jesus said: "Thou shalt love the Lord thy God with all thy heart, and with all thy soul, and with all thy mind"

66

(Matthew 22:37). When God becomes the very center of our affection, of our feeling, and of our thinking, we will find and possess—and be possessed by—God.

When I stand on the platform behind the pulpit, I am very sensitive to the congregation. You would be surprised if you knew how I watched the faces of the people to whom I minister, and the variety of expressions I see. At the start of a service, some are quiet in thought. Others are in prayer and seem hardly conscious of their surroundings. Some are chatting away with those around them, observing their clothes, watching those who come in as they are seated. There are some whose faces beam; I can see from their expressions that they are unaware of those about them—their focus is upon God. Then, when I begin to bring my message, there are some that I would compare to blotters or sponges, for they hear with all their senses and soak up every word that I say. There are others, however, who sit there utterly unresponsive. I am sure that they could not tell you what the sermon was about.

What really makes the difference? It is simply this— there are some who thirst after righteousness and hunger for God; they truly desire spiritual food. On the other hand, there are those who are indifferent and expect the Lord to put it into their pocket without any effort on their part.

Through the years I have observed that one will never find God until God becomes the deepest desire of that individual. One gets exactly what he is looking for! He will see what he wants to see. He will find in life what he really wants to find. Jesus knew human nature; therefore,

He could say, "Blessed are they which do hunger and thirst after righteousness: for they shall be filled." *Thirst* is a strong word, and when a human soul thirsts for God, that soul will be filled with God. Not only will he find God for himself, but he will bring God's Kingdom on Earth.

This is very real to me for I cannot remember a time in my life when every atom of my being did not cry out for God. You speak of physical hunger, and I'll admit that I have been physically hungry for food; but I tell you of a truth, I have never known a physical hunger as great as my hunger for spiritual things. My hunger for salvation was marvelous, and I found satisfaction in Jesus in that little Methodist Church in Concordia, Missouri. But that was not the end of my hunger. As great as that hunger was, there was yet a greater hunger that gripped me, a hunger so great that I would look up into the heavens at night, beyond the shining stars, and say, "I know I belong to you, Jesus, but I hunger after a greater and deeper experience. I have only tasted and I have only glimpsed into what You have prepared for me. Please, wonderful Jesus, give me more. Fill every part of me until this body of mine has become a yielded vessel filled to overflowing with the Holy Spirit."

It was not one experience or some evidence that I sought. I sought more of Jesus. I sought the Giver. I had had a glimpse of His love, His might, His power and I wanted more of the one that I saw. I had had a taste, but I wanted more of that which I had tasted. Jesus promised, "Blessed is he who hungers and thirsts;" and the Holy Spirit came to me and did appease that hunger and craving, and did satisfy my thirst.

I do not believe that there is a limit to Jesus' giving, and as you hunger and thirst after His presence and surrender yourself to Him and His will, your longings will be satisfied and you will experience, as I did, the glories of God's filling, the thrill of His power, and the nearness of His indwelling presence.

FIVE

God's Great Mercy

"Blessed are the merciful." You know, of all the ways and the means that afford us access to God's Kingdom, this one is the most attractive, the most vital, and to many of us, the most troublesome at times. First of all, it is attractive because mercy reminds us of unselfish service, of kindness, of goodness, of goodwill. As human beings, we draw back from the thought of God's justice, and are reluctant to think of Him in terms of justice. All of us pray for His mercy and we long for His mercy to be poured out upon us in fullest measure. It is not His justice that we seek but His mercy. Without mercy—we are sunk. Every one of us has sinned and come short of God's glory, and the only prayer that you and I can pray is, "God be merciful to me a sinner." Why? Because without His mercy, there is nothing left but justice, and justice demands God's judgment because we are sinners. Each one of us, therefore, desires and prays for His mercy.

But watch something. Even though we long for God's mercy and plead for His forbearance, it is one of the most difficult of all character traits for us as human beings, because despite our desire for mercy, it is not an easy assignment to sincerely extend mercy to another.

There is seldom a church service on the Lord's Day that the congregation fails to stand and together pray what is called "The Lord's Prayer." Sometimes I think we should not stop with that verse in Matthew 6:13, but continue our prayer through the fourteenth and fifteenth verses because they are very vital to our healthy Christian life. "If ye forgive men their trespasses, your heavenly Father will also forgive you" (Matthew 6:14).

It is agreed that we all want God's forgiveness, and we all want the forgiveness of our fellow man. You want your wife to forgive you. You want your husband to forgive you. You want all of the neighbors to forgive you of your shortcomings regardless of what they are. You want the folk where you work to forgive you. You want society to forgive you in spite of your wrongs; and you pray daily that God will forgive your weaknesses, your failures, and your sins.

The 15th verse takes you a step further: "If ye forgive not men their trespasses, neither will your Father forgive your trespasses." Thousands of people pray the prayer that Jesus taught—The Lord's Prayer—but only a few are familiar with and pray this part of the prayer. This thing of forgiveness is two-fold. If you want forgiveness, you must forgive. If you want God to forgive your sins, you will have to forgive your fellow men their sins.

Now some will say, "I cannot forgive because I was right and the other party was wrong. Why should I forgive?" But consider the fact that in asking God to forgive you your sins, you were wrong and God was right. Even the word sin means that you were wrong in what you did. God forgave you your wrongs when He forgave your sins, and He continues to be a forgiving heavenly Father as you bring your sins before Him and ask His forgiveness. God is merciful in forgiving; therefore, you and I must be just as merciful in forgiving others their sins whether or not they were right or wrong in what they did. It is not ours to judge. We must be merciful in forgiving.

Do you want to know something? The most expensive thing that you can do is to hold a wrong spirit in your heart against someone else—I do not care who that one is. There is nothing that is more costly to an individual.

If you carry a grudge or an unforgiving spirit in your heart against someone else, your body can be affected. The amusing thing is that this does not bother the other person at all. He may not even know of the vengeful spirit that is there in your heart. For example, you would be amazed how many write to me and say: "Miss Kuhlman, I have to make a confession. I took exception to something you said or something that you did, and I have been holding that in my heart against you."

Seldom do I know that person and all the time he harbored unforgiveness in his heart, I was totally unaware of it. It did not affect me one bit. I had gone right on with my life as though that person with his grudge never existed, but it was mighty expensive to that one because it hindered his spiritual growth. It hindered the healing of his soul. It kept him from being used by God in a more powerful way. It could even have kept

God from answering prayer, because God cannot bless a human being who is not willing to forgive. That is why I believe that to hold a wrong spirit in one's heart against someone else is one of the most expensive things that a person can do.

We read in Matthew 18 that it was Peter who came to Jesus with a question, "How oft shall my brother sin against me, and I forgive him? Till seven times?" Peter may have thought that one time was enough, and that he was big-hearted if he forgave him a second time. Three times was far too much for Peter, but he thought he would go all the way and said, "Lord, how about seven times? Don't you think seven is enough?" Jesus replied, "I say not unto thee, Until seven times: but, until seventy times seven" (Matthew 18:21-22).

Then Jesus continues with a most important illustration, the story of the king who forgave his servant a large debt which he could not pay. Read the account for yourself as it is recorded in Matthew 18, starting with verse 23. "Therefore is the kingdom of heaven likened unto a certain king, which would take account of his servants. And when he had begun to reckon, one was brought unto him, which owed him ten thousand talents." Just think of the size of the debt, millions of dollars by today's standards. It was a debt that would be absolutely impossible to pay.

But forasmuch as he had not to pay, his lord commanded him to be sold, and his wife, and children, and all that he had, and payment to be made. The servant therefore fell down, and worshipped him, saying, Lord, have patience

74

with me, and I will pay thee all. Then the lord of that servant was moved with compassion, and loosed him, and forgave him the debt." He did not have to repay a nickel. He forgave the whole debt and wrote across the account, "Paid in full!" Mercy forgave!

But the same servant [the one who had been forgiven] went out, and found one of his fellowservants, which owed him an hundred pence [only a few dollars, that is all]: and he laid hands on him, and took him by the throat, saying, Pay me that thou owest. And his fellowservant fell down at his feet, and besought him, saying, Have patience with me, and I will pay thee all. And he would not: but went and cast him into prison, till he should pay the debt. So when his fellowservants saw what was done, they were very sorry, and came and told unto their lord all that was done. Then his lord, after that he had called him, said unto him, O thou wicked servant, I forgave thee all that debt, because thou desirest me: Shouldest not thou also have had compassion on thy fellowservant, even as I had pity on thee? And his lord was wroth, and delivered him to the tormentors, till he should pay all that was due unto him." Jesus continues by saying, "So likewise shall my heavenly Father do also unto you, if ye from your hearts forgive not everyone his brother their trespasses."

How does one show mercy? How does one forgive? Many a man has buried the hatchet, but he lets the handle stick out of the soil so he can grab it any time he wants to use it again. I have seen two men bury the hatchet and shake hands. For the moment it is wonderful, but one of them lets the handle of the hatchet stick out. Six months pass, then something happens. He is reminded of his grudge and he grabs the old handle and wields the hatchet again.

Unless you forgive the one who has hurt you, it is impossible for Jesus to forgive you of your sins. He withholds His mercy until you are willing to show mercy to that brother, to that sister, to that person who has wronged you. You may have every reason to feel offended. You may be absolutely right, but that is where mercy comes in. That is what the word means. It is only mercy that can forgive a wrong.

How does one forgive? With the lips only? Not on your life! God does not forgive like that. When God forgives our sins, He not only forgives, He forgets to remember those sins against us any longer. He erases our sins that we confess. He blots them out of His memory so that if we come back after confessing our sins and ask for forgiveness of those sins again, God will not know what we are talking about because He blotted them out of His memory. He erased them from His mind because He forgave from the heart.

"If ye forgive not men their trespasses, neither will your Father forgive your trespasses" (Matthew 6:15). That is why I say the most expensive thing you can do is to hold a wrong spirit in your heart against another. Instead, God honors a merciful heart, and the merciful never lose a battle!

SIX

The Pure in Heart

" Blessed are the pure in heart: for they shall see God." I am intrigued by the promise Jesus gives us here—they shall see God. Let's be practical about this thing. In using the word "see," we note that one's vision is involved, and none will dispute that the sight of the human eye is something very marvelous. So often you have heard me say to you, "If you have two good eyes, you are rich. You have something that money cannot buy. One's vision is a wonderful thing."

But I am sure you are fully aware that all people do not possess the same ability to see. As a child, I can remember my elation when Mama would call me and say, "Kathryn, would you please thread this needle for me?" You see, practically every night after the supper dishes were done, Mama would do a little sewing, a little mending, a little crocheting, or put some lace on a new dress. It pleased me when she would call for my help in threading her needle, because I could do something that Mama could not do for herself. Besides, it assured me that my eyesight was a little better than Mama's. In those days, it was no trick at all for me to pass the thread through the smallest eye of a needle.

Now my point is this. All people do not have the same ability to see. Many have distorted or limited vision because of a variety of eye problems. Some are nearsighted, some farsighted. Therefore, regarding this thing we call vision, we note that all people do not view the same thing in the same way as they look at an object.

For example, when I was in Vienna, I asked to see the River Danube. I was expecting it to be the most beautiful river in all the world, blue as the Mediterranean, clear as the water of Crater Lake in the State of Oregon. I'll admit that I was disappointed, for it seemed as dirty and muddy as the Missouri River at home! Yet, somebody else in looking at it saw the beautiful blue Danube. We were looking at the identical river, but he and I did not *see* it in the same way.

Another example is this—recently there has been a great move of God among the youth, and I have been taking a personal interest in these young men and women. There have been those who have questioned, "How can you tolerate some of those characters?" My answer is simply this; I do not see them in the light of what they are now. I see them in the light of what they can be in God, when He places His hand on them and transforms their lives. I see beyond their drug addiction. I see beyond their sordid lives. I see beyond the filth and the sin and I see them in the light of what they can be in Christ. By faith, I can see a new creature in Jesus. I can see a life transformed by His power. I can see a young person who is a power for God.

There is the alcoholic living on the street. If I saw that man only as he appears before me, I would not take the time to talk with him or to pray for or with him. Seeing him as he is, there is nothing that can be done for him. He is a hopeless case. But because I see what he can be when his life is transformed by the power of Almighty God, I have patience with him, pray with and for him, and take time to deal with him.

Somebody may label my vision as farsighted. But on the other hand, I know a lot of people who are mighty nearsighted, so nearsighted in fact, that unless their vision is corrected, they can never see beyond themselves and that which touches their lives.

Follow me very closely now. There are at least three ways in which all of us see. Paul describes them perfectly. "Eye hath not seen, nor ear heard, neither have entered into the heart of man, the things which God hath prepared for them that love him" (1 Corinthians 2:9).

The three kinds of sight considered here are: natural, mental, and spiritual. There is the sight of the natural eye with which we see the flowers, the mountains and objects about us, including the printed page and people's faces. It is physical vision that we are acquainted with and possess to some degree.

Let's go a little deeper. A teacher explains a problem in mathematics, chemistry, etc.—as the teacher speaks, the student hears. He may not see a thing with his natural vision, but he hears, and his mind takes hold of what he hears to the point of understanding. After he understands he will say, "I see it." Yet, with his physical vision, he may not have seen a thing. He heard with his ears, his mind took hold of what he heard to the point of understanding, and he saw. What kind of sight is this? It is different from physical vision. It is a mental sight. In studying a given subject on the printed page, a student sees with both his mind and his eyes because he understands what he reads.

Now we will consider the facts about a third sight which I consider the most important of the three sights that man can possess. I know that good physical vision is something very valuable and a priceless gift. You also will agree that this sight through the ear and mind is marvelous. But I think this third sight, the sight of the heart, is the most priceless of all.

That is what Paul is talking about in his letter to the Corinthian believers, as he states, "neither hath entered into the heart of man, the things which God hath prepared for them that love him," The heart has eyes too; I pray that God will not only preserve my physical and mental vision, but keep the vision of my heart intact as well. Jesus looked at people and had compassion on them. And what was that marvelous compassion? Was it really the sight of His eyes? Of course He saw them with His eyes and mind, but He also saw with His heart—that is what real compassion is.

A person sees God through the eyes of the heart. There is no other way that you and I can see God as long as we are in these bodies of flesh. When a person tells you that he has seen God, that he has actually and literally looked upon the person of God, that one does not speak truth, for the Scripture says that no man can look upon God and live (Exodus 33:20). You and I are in these bodies of flesh that are yet corruption, and that which is yet mortal cannot look upon the person of God Almighty. These bodies of ours, in the condition as they are today, cannot look upon the absolute perfection and holiness of God and live.

Paul was a great spiritual giant, but as long as Paul was in his body of flesh, he could never say that he looked upon the person of Almighty God with his physical eyes. Why? Because these natural bodies of ours are not geared for absolute holiness and purity, and with our mortal eyes we cannot look upon the face of God.

Many have asked me if I have seen God. No, not really, and yet through the eyes of my heart, I have seen the one who is my heavenly Father. He is as real to me as the air I breathe. My natural eyes have not seen Jesus, but through the eyes of my heart, He is as real to me as though I have seen Him and looked on His face.

Therefore, it may seem to be a contradiction when we read this part of the eighth verse of this fifth chapter of Matthew that states, "they shall see God," for we know we cannot see Him while in these mortal bodies. Oh sure, there is coming a day when you and I are going to stand in His wonderful presence. We are going to look upon His face. We will rejoice in His presence. There isn't a doubt in my mind that one of these days I will see my heavenly Father. Nobody can ever talk me out of this fact. I know Him. My confidence is in Him. He is real to my heart and I am going to see Him. Yet, this sermon that Jesus preached deals with our life here and now and has nothing to do whatsoever with our life after death. He is talking about something that relates to us while we are still in the flesh, while we are living in this body that is corrupt and mortal.

Yes, on the surface it almost looks as though Jesus' words are a contradiction as He says that "they shall see God," and He meant we could see Him in this lifetime. When Phillip said to Jesus, "Show us the Father," Jesus answered: "He that hath seen me hath seen the Father" (John 14:9). Philip and those other disciples to whom He was speaking had not seen God the Father. Jesus was saying, however: Look upon Me, see Me, and through the eyes of the heart look even beyond Me and see the Father. To see God in Christ, one must experience Him in the heart; the man who has never had that spiritual experience in his heart, can possess no spiritual sight because one does not see the spiritual with physical eyes.

Neither can the mind understand heart reasoning. That is why one with perfect physical vision and a keen intellect can read the Bible and yet he will close its cover and say, "The whole thing is beyond my understanding. I do not comprehend it." There is nothing wrong with his physical vision. There is nothing wrong with the eyes of his mind. His mentality is clear. He understands the writings of the philosophers and the texts of many scholars, yet when it comes to the Bible, he reads it with his eyes alone. In spite of his keen intellect, he still has no spiritual perception or understanding, for his spiritual eyesight is nil. To see God in Christ, to see spiritual things, to see the very Son of the living God, to see and understand the things of the Spirit, one must have a *spiritual* experience in his heart. When the heart sees Christ, then we see God.

Yes, when the heart gets right—then you will see God. You will see Him in a way beyond the vision of the mind and the physical vision that enables us to read about Him. You will know in whom you have placed your confidence. Then you can come before His throne assured that you have a hearing, that underneath all the uncertainties of today and tomorrow and all the tomorrows that follow are His everlasting arms. You will know Him as a person and feel His glorious presence surrounding you.

How we see God depends on the condition of the heart. Now the Bible states that the heart of man is desperately wicked (Jeremiah 17:9). So how can one regain purity of heart and a cleansing of his soul in order that he might see God?

Here's how! In the eighth chapter of the Gospel of John, we read of the woman taken in adultery. She was caught in the very act of sin. She had no argument whatsoever. They dragged her through the streets into the presence of Jesus Christ. That day she came in contact with Him, who is the purest of the pure. She came face-to-face with Jesus and looked full into His wonderful face. Not only was she seeing Him with her physical sight, not only was she hearing His words with her ears, but His words were making contact with her mind as well. And, finally, for the first time in her life, she was seeing with her heart. Jesus looked upon her and saw her with His physical eyes, but He did not stop there. He saw her through the eyes of His own heart and He had compassion. She, in that moment, so loved Him with her heart that all of her affection was poured out on Him. She completely took Him to heart and her evil desires were cast out. Being filled with the purity of Christ—she became pure. That wonderful new-birth experience took place and she became a new creature in Christ Jesus. Old things passed away and all things became new.

Some label it the *new-birth* experience, others term it *regeneration*, but whatever title it is given, it is an inner experience. In this instance, a harlot became a virgin again in God's sight, for purity had been regained as she became a new creature in Christ Jesus. What made the difference? I will tell you. She had become pure in heart through the blood of Jesus Christ, and with purity of heart she was able to see God. "Blessed are the pure in heart: for they shall see God."

Beloved, you do not need to wait until your heart ceases to beat, until death comes to your mortal body, before you see God. You can see God now—through the spiritual eyes of your heart.

SEVEN

Peacemakers

" **B**lessed are the peacemakers: for they shall be called the children of God." Just consider for a moment this thing of being a peacemaker. The true meaning of peace as Jesus meant it here is often misunderstood. He was not referring to one who plays the role of peacemaker—bargaining or negotiating between neighbors or family members or even employees in the work place. This is not what was in Jesus' mind when He brought that message about peacemakers.

What did Jesus mean? A noted spiritual leader made this statement and I cannot find better words to express how I define the peace Jesus intended to convey in this portion of Scripture. I quote from this man's comments: "Peace is not the absence of war, but the tranquility of order. Order is the subordination of senses to reason, body to soul; reason to faith, the whole personality to God. Peace is not automatic; it is made."

World leaders have tried, and are still trying through their own efforts and through legislation, to bring peace to the world, but despite their diligent endeavors and the many hours spent working toward that end, they will never achieve a peaceful world.

Then how is it gained? It must come by inner regeneration. Only he who has the peace of God in his own soul can give it to others. Perhaps you have noticed, as I have, that this thing of peace is the most sought after thing in the world. There is not a sensible and intelligent person living today who does not want peace in the world. Everybody wants worldwide peace. Books galore have been written on the subject of peace, and as quickly as they leave the publishers' presses they sell millions of copies. People everywhere are seeking for peace in their minds and peace in their own individual lives. Peace today is at a premium.

If you have ever tuned in my radio talks, you may have heard me speak these few lines of verse that are very meaningful to me:

I went to see a wise old man
And he was very kind,
What is life's sweetest gift, I asked;
He answered, Peace of mind.
When I met a great physician,
I was quite surprised to find,
That he thought the finest medicine;
Was simply peace of mind.
And so I pass this on to friends;
Who would leave all gloom behind,
The key to life's great mysteries,
Consists of peace of mind.

Peace is vitally important. I'm sure it is one of the reasons why Jesus included peacemakers in His Sermon on the Mount, and why He said in John 14:27: "Peace I leave with you, my peace I give unto you."

What exactly is the peace that Jesus promised to leave with His disciples, that He will give to us? We all agree that peace is important, but important as it is, as earnestly as it is desired, and as fervently as nations seem to strive for it, I wonder if many fully understand exactly what peace is.

It is my opinion that even our wisest men do not have a true conception of it. Billions and billions of dollars have been spent trying to obtain peace, which is a noble endeavor, and it is often analyzed and debated, but do we really understand? It is more than ridding hatred from the hearts of mankind. The prejudice, suspicion, and fear within our fellowmen is heart-rending. But even if we could remove these and other base character traits from human hearts by inoculating them with some kind of serum, we still would not solve the problem.

Peace is a vital and positive force, one that perhaps I can best explain by giving you an illustration. Let's suppose you have a little plot of ground in your back yard or at the side of your house, where you plan a flower garden. The best way to do it effectively, you say to yourself, is to rid the soil of all weeds. So you begin to work long and hard until every weed on that little plot of ground has been wiped out. There isn't a weed left and you feel so satisfied. Now, you say, because I have destroyed the weeds that were on that plot of ground, I have a beautiful flower garden. Wrong! Even though you have destroyed the weeds, you do not have a flower garden. All that you have is a barren plot of ground. You have done away with the weeds, but it will only become a garden when flowers are growing there—the flowers must be planted. A garden does not sprout automatically.

Peace, also, is not automatic. It is something that is generated. To make my point still a little clearer, let me go a bit further. The prophet (Micah 4:3) states that we must go beyond breaking up the swords and spears that comprise our weapons. They must be fashioned into plowshares and pruning hooks. To have peace, both in the world and in our hearts, hate, suspicion, and fear must be rooted out, and in their stead love, joy, understanding, patience, and mercy must be planted and cultivated. We must set our minds upon the positive and not the negative. We will never have love, understanding, mercy, or real joy unless these things are planted and cultivated in our lives.

Removing the weeds alone does not make a flower garden. You will never have a flower garden unless you plant the seeds. In the same way, after the hate and prejudice have been removed from a human heart, one must plant and cultivate understanding, love, patience, and mercy.

In the third chapter of Mark, the twenty-fifth verse, we find a very familiar portion of Scripture, "If a house be divided against itself, that house cannot stand." There are three ways by which a life is divided, and if you are living any one of these three divided lives, you do not, you cannot, you will not, have peace of mind or peace of soul.

First, we will examine the divided self-life, divided between its inner self and its outer self. You and I have an inner self and an outer self, since we are a part of humanity; and within most of us, there is that conflict between the inner and the outer self. The Pharisees, as depicted in the Bible, are a good example of that divided life. Everything they said and did in public was a display to be seen of men. They tried to act the part of saints and to be very religious on the outside, even praying long prayers where they could be seen and heard. What they did was not because they were righteous on the inside, not because of their sincerity, not because of a love God had instilled within them, but it was a front to be seen of men. They sought to display an outward something that was wholly contrary to what they felt and were on the inside—and thus they were hypocrites.

The world is no different today. It is loaded with hypocrites, and many of them can be found in our churches, sad to say. Have you wondered why we are not seeing our altars filled with men and women seeking to know Christ? Do you want to know why the unsaved person has little confidence in the average professing Christian? It's because he knows that, for the most part, the professing Christians are no better than he is. He sees them. He works with them. He knows what they are like. Jesus would class them in the same category with the hypocrites of His day here on earth. I'll be honest with you and say if your inside is not like your outside then you are nothing but a hypocrite, and you are experiencing a terrific battle between the inner and the outer man, because you are trying to be two persons.

I cannot hold with the idea believed by some folk, that many good people's children go bad. There are some exceptions, of course, but in general, I do not believe it. Perhaps you too have heard the account of the mother who took her little boy to the zoo. In looking at the animals, he spotted one that was unfamiliar to him. He asked,

"What is that one?"

His mother replied, "That is a wildcat."

His next question was, "Mama, what are those little ones in there with the wildcat?"

"Those are little wildcats," she answered.

Like produces like. That youngster who is uncontrollable, that child who is a delinquent, is most often a little wildcat because he has wildcats for parents.

All of us have met those who appear to be the most pious and lovable, grandest and politest, folk in the world—that is, to the people on the street. But to those at home, they are nothing short of beasts. If you want to know whether or not a man is really a Christian and lives that life, do not ask his pastor. Ask his wife. Ask his children. And if your life on the inside is not what you display to the outside world, then I beg you to stop and start all over again—now. Do not make a profession of Christianity or pretend to be something that you're not. If you are trying to be two people living a life that is divided between an inner and an outer self, you are living a lie and you cannot have peace of mind and peace in your soul.

In your search for peace, you can read a library of books on the subject. You can carefully study all the aspects of peace. You can digest the philosophies of the most learned scholars, but until you look at yourself and realize that you are trying to live two lives, trying to be two people, you will not know or experience peace of mind and soul. Be honest with yourself. Be dead honest and say, "From here on out I am going to be the same person at home that I am on the street. I will be the same person on Monday through Saturday, that I am on Sunday." Many a man hangs his religion next to his Sunday suit after church.

Then, until he reaches for that Sunday suit and puts it on the next week, he lives like the devil and wonders why he does not have peace of mind and peace of soul.

What did Jesus say in the third chapter of Mark? He said that if your house, your temple, you personally—if that house is divided against itself, that house cannot stand.

The second way that a life is divided is by the forward and backward look. You may not know what I mean by that, but hear me out. When God created man in His own image and after His likeness, He created man with a forward look, with a pair of eyes that would constantly be looking forward and not backward. By looking backward instead of forward, we bring on ourselves much of our distress, our unhappiness, our frustration, our confusion, our lack of peace.

Some people have not looked forward for many years. I know a woman who has not looked forward since the day of her husband's death. She is still living in the memory of that one who died twenty years ago.

Then, there is the precious mother who has not looked forward since the day her child died. She has constantly had the backward look, and it doesn't surprise me that she has no joy, peace of mind, or peace of soul. Why? Because no human being was created for the backward look. We were made to look forward.

Too many of us do just the opposite. We are forever thinking backward instead of forward. It seems the easiest thing in the world to live in the past. When we live in the past, there are and will be regrets. We see the nurturing of hurt feelings. There will be thoughts of injustice, there will be memories of things that should be buried and forgotten. We are reluctant to loose our hold on the past and hesitate to start living the future. As a result, instead of joy and adventure, we know only the pangs of remorse, and we never have peace of mind.

It seems that some people cannot let go of the past. You've met them too and sometimes when I see them coming and I know that they will be part of the group, I sigh within myself because I know exactly what the conversation will be—every word will be negative and about the past. Even a subject that seems totally unrelated will trigger a negative statement. They have lived with a backward look for so long that it is almost impossible for them to look forward. Therefore, they are living without joy and without adventure.

If I have described your life in the foregoing statement, I must warn you that you will never in a thousand worlds know or have peace of soul until you bury the past and start living for the future. There is a day in every week about which we should never worry, and that day is yesterday: yesterday with its mistakes and cares, and with its faults and its blunders. With its aches, its pains, and its sorrows yesterday is gone. It is gone forever.

I would have lived a life of defeat if I had been satisfied to live in the yesterdays of my life. Sometimes I do not think anybody has made more mistakes than I have made. Oh, those mistakes! And when I blunder, they are big blunders! I have never trifled with little things, even in my mistakes. If I had stopped looking forward each time I made a mistake and had started living with a backward look, I would never be where I am today. I did not move forward in my life until I was willing to cover those tragic blunders and mistakes with the blood of Jesus Christ. And I do that today! Instead of wallowing in remorse over my mistakes, I ask God's forgiveness. I put on His glasses. Then, looking through His lenses, I have the forward look. My focus is not on what has been, my eyes are on a future goal. I am looking ahead, and my mind is centered on what I can do for God tomorrow.

Therefore, beloved, I have learned that it is not the experience of today that drives one mad; but the remorse and the bitterness of yesterday that one still clings to and holds in his grasp. No person will ever have peace of mind and peace of soul if he is still living yesterday's problems and mistakes, instead of fixing his sights on tomorrow's possibilities and attainable triumphs.

There is still a third way that a life is divided, and that is by the higher and the lower natures. Let me give you an example. I was very young when I started to preach and one of my earliest sermons was regarding Elijah as recorded in I Kings 18. Even as a teenager, this message appealed to me and made a deep and lasting impression upon my life.

Picture Elijah as he stood before the people on Mount Carmel and pleaded with them. I do not know if he was pleading with them in exasperation or challenging them; but I do know what he said to them: "How long halt ye between two opinions?" (verse 21). In other words Elijah was saying: "How long are you going to remain in the state of indecision? Make up your minds! If the Lord is God, follow Him. But if Baal is god, then follow him. Do one of two things, but make up your minds—what you are going to do? If you choose to follow God, and if God is everything that He claims to be, then go all out for God. If you choose to follow Baal, then pack up your glad rags and follow him. But please make up your minds and stop your wavering and your indecision."

In the epistle written by James, we read that "he that wavereth is like a wave of the sea driven with the wind and tossed. For let not that man think that he shall receive anything of the Lord" (James 1:6-7). Any person who remains in a state of indecision never gets anything from God, never accomplishes anything, and never amounts to anything.

The first thing that you must do if you are going to be a successful Christian is to determine to stand firm for God, no matter what happens, no matter what comes, no matter how deep the waters, no matter how severe the fight, no matter how great the battle. Your first requisite as a Christian is your unwavering determination to follow God. You must make up your mind. God forbid that we should stand in indecision.

There is an inner peace that fills one who completely decides for God, but the one who is undecided, who rides the rail, who wavers with the changing days, lives a life of misery and torment. That one will get no place with God. Ambition is not enough. Behind ambition must be determination.

Two thousand years ago Jesus said that "No man can serve two masters" (Matthew 6:24). Yet, we have not learned our lesson. Do you want peace of mind? Do you want that wonderful inner peace that passes all understanding? God's peace goes far beyond your comprehension. When you cannot understand, when you cannot see, there remains an inner peace of mind and a peace of soul that no outer conflict can shake or disturb. Is that what you desire? Then make your decision once and for all to serve God and to serve Him alone.

EIGHT

Persecuted for Righteousness' Sake

In previous chapters, we have examined seven qualities of character that concern our lives as Christians, a pattern of the Kingdom of God on Earth; and now we come to the eighth: "Blessed are they which are persecuted for righteousness' sake: for theirs is the Kingdom of Heaven."

It is apparent here that it will cost something if we are to live as Christians, but unless these qualities of character are translated into everyday living, they are absolutely worthless.

I am going to pause for just a minute to say something that may seem unrelated to the subject, but it will help you understand a vitally important truth. You know, whenever it comes to the things of God, people get ethereal in their thinking. The average man's concept of God amazes me. He thinks of God as one interested in the spiritual side of life only. He acknowledges the fact that God is a wonderful Creator, and he sees His power in action as "nature at work." Yet, I am convinced that God is very different from what we think Him to be.

Do you realize that God is interested in the life of each of us? You are important to Him. I am important to Him. He has promised us eternal life after death, but we need not wait until death comes to enjoy our inheritance in Christ Jesus. You and I have a wonderful future here on Earth. He has a plan for our pleasure, for our daily living, for our enjoyment of those things that He has prepared for us here and now on this Earth.

I am convinced that it was never in God's plan that any of His children should be beggars, or poverty-stricken, or live a defeated life. I get disgusted—and I make no apologies for using that word—with men and women who profess to be born-again children of God, yet live such defeated lives. If all that I knew about God and spiritual things was the example set by some folk who are professing Christians, I would never be a Christian. There is nothing about their lives that is challenging or positive or beautiful. There is nothing about their walk with God that leads me to believe that He is alive, that He has all power in Heaven and Earth, that He is the mighty Conqueror. How can their heavenly Father be the all-powerful God of this universe when they, as His children, live such defeated lives? If you meet these people on the street, the first thing that you hear is a long list of all their difficulties and the trials that are theirs. To be honest with you, without an audible word, I can see defeat written across their faces; and by their attitude, it would appear that God died.

You may accuse me of bordering on being sacrilegious, but I believe it is those who are living such defeated lives, who are the sacrilegious ones. They have failed to claim that which Jesus bought and paid for as a part of their inheritance. When we are born again, when we accept Christ as our Savior and become Christians, the mighty God of this universe automatically becomes our heavenly Father. It is a fact that at that moment we become heirs of God and joint-heirs with God's Son.

What would you think of someone who suddenly inherited a sizable legacy, and as a result had a million dollars at his disposal; yet he refused to withdraw a penny from that account? He allowed all those resources to remain dormant in the bank, and went around in defeat and despair, beaten and hungry. The clothing on his back was torn. He continued to live in a hovel, and his neighbors felt nothing but pity for him because of his extreme poverty.

But he wasn't poor! He was rich! In his own right he was a millionaire, having received a legacy worth a million dollars. Every penny of it was his, but he lived a poverty-stricken life because he was not drawing on the account that was rightfully his. Because he refused to claim that which was his, he remained poor.

If you are a Christian, you are somebody in the sight of God. You are an heir of God. Walk over and look at yourself in the mirror right now. Do you look like one of the King's children and an heir of God? Do you act like a child of the King? Would His heir talk the way you talk, or live in defeat as you are living?

This thing of living a Christian life is the most practical thing in the world. God never ordained that even the least of His children should live a life of defeat, despondency, or depression. Do you understand why I wish that I could remove the word "depressed" from the human vocabulary? If you say that you belong to God's kingdom and that you are one of His children, I challenge you to start drawing on that which is rightfully yours. Square your shoulders and say these four words, *"... and I am His."*

I will never forget the day when I discovered those four words in the Song of Solomon, chapter 2, verse 16: "AND I AM HIS." Confidentially, I have had to practice what I preach, and I am taking the lid off my heart as I share some things with you now. In reality it is very simple, so I urge you to try it, if you will.

You see, my responsibilities are tremendous, and the load I carry gets mighty heavy sometimes. When you need prayer, you come to me or go to your pastor. But when I need prayer, I have no one to go to but God himself. I carry the responsibility of this ministry. I have many problems to face, and there are times when I awaken in the middle of the night, and the full weight of my burden and the load that I am carrying presses upon me and is very heavy. But instead of rolling and tossing in my bed, I get up. If it's summer time, I go to my backyard where no one can see me. The only sounds may be the chirp of a cricket and the peep of a tiny bird. In the darkness of the night, I look up. I spread my arms apart, as far apart as I can. I square my shoulders. I stand straight as I look up. I lift my face. I breathe as deeply as I can breathe, and I say, "AND I AM HIS!" I say it out loud.

Perhaps you cannot go to your backyard, but you can stand in the middle of your kitchen or living room, or right there in your bedroom. Look up. Say these four words audibly: *"And I am His."* Say them again. Repeat them until they become a vital part of your being. You do not merely belong to the Kingdom of God, but the Kingdom of God belongs to you because you are His. You need not worry. You have nothing to fear. You are not carrying your load alone. God knows you cannot carry it alone; you would break under the weight of your burden. Those problems are really not your problems. They are God's. As a result, you can turn around, go to your bed, lie down, and go to sleep. You have shifted the responsibility over to God, to One who is your heavenly Father.

Yes, you will have problems and difficulties. There will be adversaries, and there will be conflicts. There will be a warfare in your life as a Christian but remember something: Jesus never promised ease to those who follow Him. He never promised a bed of roses to those who would dare to accept Him. He did talk about self-denial and a cross and a cup. He talked about a battlefield and warfare. To enter the Kingdom of God may mean decisions that are hard, a consecration that may lead to persecution but it can be no other way.

When that mother came to Jesus on one occasion in behalf of her two sons, she made a request that her sons would sit on either side of Him in His kingdom (Matthew 20:21-22). Jesus' reply in effect was, "It is not mine to give seats. If you follow Me, there is no time to sit. Instead, here is a cup. Instead, here is a cross. If any man will come after Me, let him deny himself."

Jesus talked of self-denial, of death-dealing crosses. To enter the Kingdom of God means making decisions, it involves consecration, and those decisions and that consecration may lead to persecution. "Let him deny himself, and take up his cross, and follow me" (Matthew 16:24).

Smyrna was given the command: "Be thou faithful unto death" (Revelation 2:10). The Lord Jesus meant that we are to be faithful, not merely until death, but UNTO death. My way of expressing this same command is simply: Be faithful until it kills you! Be faithful not only when the going is easy and while the sun is shining, but faithful under all circumstances.

That is why some people appear to live an inconsistent Christian life. While in church they can lick the world. They sing a little louder than anyone else. They testify a little longer than anyone else. They talk a little more than anyone else. But something happens to them between the time they leave the church service and Monday morning. Something has leaked out along the way. If you see them Monday evening, the glory has been wiped from their faces. Their smile is gone. Their shoulders are stooped.

Jesus Christ said that we are to be faithful if it kills us. Faithful no matter how deep the waters, regardless of the persecution. The very first time persecution comes to some people, they lose the victory. I believe, with every atom of my being, that no person really lives until he has found something worth dying for. We must have a purpose and a goal in life. We must find something that is worth living for and dying for. Some folk go through life eking out an existence from one day to the next, and eventually, they are satisfied with the government keeping them. They have no real purpose.

I will share something with you that few people know, just to prove a point. Some time ago, I was on the air and a man representing a large internationally known business concern, walked into the radio station. He could not see me and had no idea who I was, but he heard my voice as I was broadcasting. Turning to the manager of the station he said, "Our company will buy that woman. Let her name her price. She is the best saleswoman that I have ever heard. Whoever she is, get her and let her name her price!"

He never dreamed I was a preacher. I laughed when the manager of the radio station related the incident to me. Why did I laugh? Because I know that I am the poorest salesperson that anyone ever saw. That businessman believed I was a super salesperson simply because I am sold on the product that I am selling.

Yes, I am sold on the Lord Jesus Christ! I am sold on the Word of God! I am sold on what I believe! I have found something that is worth dying for. You can never really possess the Kingdom of God until the cause of God becomes more important to you than your own life. Believe me. That is true. You will never know the thrill, the challenge, the fullness of your inheritance until the cause of Christ becomes more important than your own life. Jesus will never become completely real to you and you can never really possess this wonderful Kingdom of God that Jesus talked about in this great sermon, until God and the things of God become more important to you than your own life.

NINE

Salt and Light

We are nearing the end of this series on the fifth chapter of Matthew, but I think there is something we often fail to see: that we cannot separate the first eleven or twelve verses of this fifth chapter from the remainder of the great sermon that Jesus preached that day. I know, whenever we think of this portion of Scripture we see it in the light of the first eleven or twelve verses, and we call that portion of Jesus' sermon, "The Beatitudes." But you must admit that the rest of the sermon that Jesus gave on that mountain is just as important as the first part of His message.

As I continue with this, you will understand exactly what I am trying to say. It is wonderful to be a Christian, but remember something beloved: to be born again is not merely an experience to be used as a fire escape. It is not to be thought of in terms of going to heaven and escaping hell. Too often, we who stand behind the pulpit make the mistake of pointing the finger at the unregenerate and saying, "If you want to go to Heaven instead of spending eternity in hell, you will have to receive Jesus Christ as your Savior." That is true, but we must not focus our sights on the distant future when our life with Christ right now is most important.

We are the sons of God now. Our life as Christians is important right here on this Earth. To be frank with you, I have so much to do for the Lord right here and now that I do not have much time to think about Heaven. Oh, I have to admit that I get homesick sometimes, especially when I think about Papa and Mama who are waiting for me there. I think of that great reunion with all my loved ones, and there is a longing within me to behold the person of Jesus, to see Him face-to-face. I suppose we all think about Heaven in that light, but I would be untruthful if I said that I am living for the day when I reach Heaven, and am conscious of the reality of Heaven every hour of my life. I am not. I have a big job right here. There is much to do for the Lord now. Heaven is there in the distant future and by the grace of God, I am going to make it one day. But I have a job to do as a part of His Church. I have work to do as a member of the body of Christ. I am His representative. My responsibilities are great. The opportunities He places before me are wonderful, and I must make every minute count.

I challenge some of you who are born-again believers to realize the tremendous responsibility that is yours NOW. Get busy for God. I mean that. This thing of being a Christian is important and if you do not think that you have a big job to do, let me bring something to your attention.

You and I—right here on this earth—are to do something that Jesus himself could not do. You may think my words border on heresy, but you will agree as you hear me out. There is no one who believes more in the power of Jesus than I do. All three persons of the Trinity were present when God spoke the world into existence. When Jesus hung on the Cross and cried, "It is finished," He could have called legions of angels to do His bidding. At His word, they would have taken Him down from that Cross. His enemies could have been smitten with death itself at Jesus' command. It was, and is, in His power to give and to take life.

Nevertheless, there was one thing that Jesus could not do. All will agree that He was perfection in its highest state. He was as much man as though He were not God, as much God as though He were not man, but sin never touched the person of the Son of God. To the question asked Him by the Jews, those who were thirsty for His very blood and who had hounded His footsteps night and day, watching His every move that they might catch Him in the smallest sin, He turned and challenged them with these words: "Which of you convinceth me of sin?" (John 8:46). Not one could lay a finger on any sin in His life, for He was absolute perfection.

Not for one split second am I belittling or taking away from Jesus Christ's mighty power, but because He was perfection and had never sinned, He could not reveal to lost sinners the transforming power of His shed blood by His own life. He could not say to the world, as they looked upon Him, that He was an example of one who had sinned, and whose life revealed the transforming power of the shed blood of God's Son. That was one thing that Jesus could not do. When He went to take His place at the Father's right hand, He left this great responsibility and privilege for you and me to do.

Our Christian testimony is the most powerful force in the life of any born-again person. If you are a born-again believer, if you are a Christian, do you realize that you may be the only Christ that the man or woman who works beside you there in that place of business ever sees? The Apostle Paul knew it and that was the reason for his words when he said, "For me to live is Christ" (Philippians 1:21). He meant that for him to walk down the street and to be associated with others is the revelation of Christ. And so I am to portray Christ to you, that you see Him in this life of mine. That is the responsibility of every Christian. We are the invisible Church of Christ.

The man on the street can see the many church buildings, places where men and women gather to worship. But there is a Church, the invisible Church, comprised of men and women who are born into that Church. They represent many denominations. "My Church," Jesus could have said, "is invisible;" and it is only as you and I live the consecrated life that we can rightfully represent His invisible Church. Beloved, never underestimate your influence as a Christian. It means much!

Turn back again to Matthew 5:13 for the continuation of Jesus' sermon masterpiece preached to the multitudes as they sat on the hillside. "Ye are the salt of the earth," He said. Yes, the throngs of people sat before Him but it is evident that these words were not addressed to them. Jesus spoke these words to the inner circle made up of those who had met the qualifications of the first part of His sermon, and to those who would meet the qualifications in the future today.

To be born again is marvelous, and that is the sole requisite for entrance into Heaven. If you have received Jesus Christ as your Savior, you will make it to heaven even if you are the weakest of Christians. But that is all. You will have lost all the joy of salvation and the thrill of being a part of the Kingdom of God right here on this Earth. You will have missed the glorious opportunities to be numbered among those called "the salt of the Earth." That is the reason I bring you back to my first statement, because you cannot separate "The Beatitudes" from the rest of Jesus' sermon.

Jesus gave "The Beatitudes" first before continuing His sermon because only as we become poor in spirit, as we learn meekness, as we become pure in heart, are we enabled to reach out to others. These are the folk who are rightfully representing the invisible Church and whose influence counts for God. You cannot be the salt of the Earth unless you are merciful, unless you are pure in heart, unless you are numbered among the peacemakers, unless you continue to hunger and thirst after righteousness.

Only as man has salt in his character can he be an influence for God to his generation. It is only as a man has light within himself that he can scatter light upon the pathway of others. It is impossible for one to give to someone else more than what he has himself.

As a minister of the Gospel, I cannot give a greater spiritual depth to members of my congregation than I have experienced myself. If you are a pastor, remember something: it isn't how well you speak or the extent of your knowledge or the degrees you have earned that will make God real to members of your congregation. When you stand behind that pulpit, you cannot give any greater spiritual depth to the members of your church than you have yourself. If God is a mystery so far as you are concerned, if you have no genuine understanding of who and what God is, if you know nothing about His power, if God is not real to you, then you cannot make Him real to your people. Jesus must be a real person to you, one who is a very vital part of your everyday living, your thinking, your breathing, and a very part of you; or you cannot make Jesus and His power real to those to whom you minister.

You see, if you have gone through the deep waters and you have felt those everlasting arms underneath as the waters were about to overflow, then the greatness of the heavenly Father's love and power is no longer a mystery to you. If you have gone through a Gethsemane and have experienced resurrection power flowing through your own life—if you have sensed the glorious presence of the Holy Spirit, then God is a reality to you and not a mystery.

So, in the same way that you can never give more to another than you have experienced yourself, neither can you exert a greater influence on another than you have experienced yourself. *The influence that you exert is always the influence of what you are.* No man exerts any influence upon another by the things he says, except as his words are an outcome and result of what he himself is in the very depth of his being.

There is something else very remarkable, and you will agree with me that it is true. There are folk whose entrance into a room brings a marked change. Prior to their presence, that room is filled with darkness. It is not a literal darkness but an unseen darkness, something you cannot quite define. There is no joy. There is no happiness.

Then, as that one enters the room, it is almost as though an electric light switch is triggered. The darkness is dispelled and you suddenly feel "light" entering the room. Why? Because within that individual there is light. One cannot give out light and cannot throw off light to those about him, unless he has the light within himself. Do you understand now what I mean?

In exactly the same way, the reverse situation occurs and is apparent to those present. There can be an almost tangible measure of happiness in a room. The very atmosphere can be alive with a presence of peace. There is no tension whatsoever, only a relaxing and peaceable atmosphere. Yet someone enters the open door and it is as though the window shades are drawn. Depression itself walks into the room because that one is depressed within, and he throws a shroud of depression upon everybody else as he comes in contact with others.

I repeat—no person exerts upon other people any great measure of influence by what he says. Only as his words are the outcome of what he is in the deepest part of his own being, does he exercise real influence upon another. The influence that you as fathers and mothers exert upon your sons and your daughters is the influence of who you are. You can talk until doomsday telling them what they should be, but your words will mean nothing if they know you are not the man or woman you are urging them to be. Therefore, you have no influence.

We are also the light of the world, and if we are not light, then we cannot shine. As we study the teaching of our Lord, we are more and more impressed with the fact that He never tarried upon the surface of a subject in His instruction. He delved down to the very depth and core. We shall never exercise the influence of salt or the influence of light to our family, to those in our church, in our town, at work, or among our neighbors, unless we are salt and light ourselves.

I know we have all smiled at this commonly cited saying, but I quote it here because it is so very true: *What you are speaks so loud that I cannot hear what you say.* The most successful Christian living today is the man or the woman who is so consecrated to God that he does not have to sell his experience. People are naturally sold on his Christianity by his life, and his influence leads them to Christ.

That is exactly what Jesus meant when He said, "Ye are the salt." What is this influence of character? The Lord made use of two figures, salt and light. He did not say, "Ye are the salt of the world." Neither did He say, "Ye are the light of the earth." This is what He did say: "Ye are the salt of the earth. Ye are the light of the world."

112

Let us look into each case and at the properties described. First, salt and earth—the one value of salt here is that its presence prevents the spread of corruption and repels the spread of impurities. Salt never changes corruption into incorruption, for salt does not have the power to change corruption into incorruption. But it does prevent corruption from spreading. Moreover, it reveals soundness and it creates the opportunity for its continuance.

There is not a man or woman or a religious leader, though deeply spiritual and greatly admired and respected, who is able to take hold of any corrupt man and make him pure. No saint who has ever lived in the past, who exists today, or will live in the future will ever possess the power to take a corrupt person and make that one pure. No man is equal to that task. That is not our work. We were not put here on this earth and we were not saved for that purpose. No human being has been given that power.

Our influence is of another value. Salt takes hold of that which is not yet corrupt and prevents its becoming corrupt. It holds back the corrupting forces and creates the opportunity for the exercise of goodness and the continuance of soundness. We are the salt, the restraining force, but Jesus is the only one who can change corruption into incorruption. Our influence is one of restraining power. Ours is not the task to change the impure and make it pure.

Those who have attended our miracle services have heard me say that I have nothing to do with the healing of the sick bodies. Yet, that one who has received healing

113

may turn to me and say, "But I would never have known how real Jesus is or the reality of His power to heal, if you had not told me of the power of Jesus." And that is the only thing that I can do. That is my part in God's great plan. I cannot make the impure become pure. I cannot change a sinful life into one that is pure and righteous or heal a sick body. That is not my work and neither is it yours. Only one has that power and that is Jesus Christ. He can take a man, whose life is besmirched by sin, and transform that life into one that is pure and righteous. He alone can give health to a sick body. But, as the salt of the Earth, we can hold back the corrupting forces of sin and unrighteousness by lifting up Christ in all of His beauty and in all of His loveliness.

Let us notice now the sphere in which salt operates, for Jesus said: "Ye are the salt of the earth." This word "earth" which Jesus used here marks the distinctly material side of things—literally, the soil. Men and women, including you and me, are of the earth. There is a practical aspect to life and Jesus knew that. He was instructing us to keep our feet anchored to the ground because of the earthly things confronting us all. We all have neighbors. We all have friends. Each of us is faced with earning a living. There are bills to be paid and other responsibilities too numerous to list. That is the reason why Jesus took the two words—salt and earth—in their true earthly meaning, and He used them as an illustration.

It is impossible for us to escape the material world. We must recognize it, but not become a part of the material to the degree that we exclude the spiritual side of living. But while we are on the Earth and have earthly needs, we are still a part of God's kingdom. We are His heirs. We have a definite work to do for Him, and He has a purpose for each of us. You and I are assigned the task to live in the midst of men and women who live under earthly and material conditions, in order to be to them an influence for Christ. We are to lead those, whose lives we touch, to the Lord by our actions and by portraying Him through the life we live. Jesus is no longer walking the streets of this Earth. He is in position of High Priest at the right hand of God the Father. Man cannot see the person of Jesus. The only Jesus the unsaved man or woman sees is through your life and mine.

In view of all the foregoing and our Lord's illustration, I'm sure you understand now why Jesus made the statement: "Ye are the salt of the earth," for your life is the medium through which the heavenly government shall operate in material things. Therefore, you are important as you live out the Christian life here in an old material world. The only power that is holding back the forces of sin, evil, and unrighteousness in the world today is the salt of the Earth that still remains, and while we are here in the world, that is our task and our responsibility.

As we consider the purpose of the very salt of the Earth and the light of the world as shown in Jesus' illustration, and as it is applied to Christians, it saddens me that not every born-again man or woman can be included in this class. It is distressing that many are weak in their Christian experience, shallow in their living, and lacking in their influence for the Lord. At one time there may have been some measure of salt there, but its savor has been lost. Their salt has lost its tang. Remember: only as one has salt in his character is it possible for that one to exercise the influence of salt. Therefore, the influence that you exert is always the influence of what you are, and only that has a lasting influence for God.

I pause here to share something personal, to lift off the lid of my heart and expose it to you. I wonder if you are like I am, always having to learn everything the hard way. I suppose that is the reason why I try so hard to shield the young people of this ministry from the heartaches and the stones that have bruised my own feet along life's way. I try the best I know to save them from some of my experiences. Oh, I'll admit that I brought them all on myself. I was to blame, but many times it was ignorance on my part, not willfulness.

In those early days of my ministry, I set out to convert the whole world. I confess that I used some tactless methods in my one-woman campaign to save the world for God. All I could preach was salvation, of course, for all I knew was that Jesus had forgiven my sins. You see, even then I realized that I could not give to anyone else any more than I had experienced myself. It was in a little country church that seated no more than two hundred people that I worked so hard at bringing the unconverted to know Jesus. The sinner that came into those services was my personal target, for if I knew he was there, I would not let him leave until I had him down on his knees. When I look back on my life now, I guess I thought I was doing the converting! Surely the Holy Spirit has been very patient and longsuffering with me.

Since that time, I have learned that I cannot change a man or woman from corruption into incorruption. I cannot convert anyone. It takes the power of God to change a life. My part is to so live that when I stand on the platform and am led to give an altar call—whether it is during the song service, before the sermon, or at the close of the meeting—that sinner will have confidence enough in my life as a Christian that I can point him to Jesus. I can lead him into the born-again experience, but Jesus is the one who does the rest! The sinner is changed by the power of God and that is exactly what Jesus was talking about when He said, "Ye are the salt of the earth." No person can take a corrupt man and make him pure, but our presence in the world will check the spread of corruption.

Now Jesus continues by saying, "Ye are the light of the world. A city that is set on a hill cannot be hid." Jesus used the present tense as He spoke: ye *are*. We are that light *now*, not after we are dead. The value of our light is illumination, a revelation of how life ought to be lived. Example is not enough to save a man, but example is a great force. Our example as a Christian will never save or convert a man, but our example is one of the greatest forces that can be exercised in our life toward the conversion of another human being. We are not called upon to save men and women. We are called upon to shine, revealing the truth of God's Word by the life that we live. Men and women living in the will of God are the light of the world. We are to live in loyalty to Christ and by so doing, we will light up the world.

117

Turn again to that fifth chapter of Matthew and read the fourteenth through the sixteenth verses. "Ye are the light of the world. A city that is set on a hill cannot be hid, neither do men light a candle, and put it under a bushel, but on a candlestick, and it giveth light unto all that are in the house. Let your light so shine before men, that they may see your good works, and glorify your Father which is in heaven."

The full explanation is very clear and simple as it is given there. Let your light shine—that is your example, something which is very personal. But you will be an example for Christ only if your character and your light measure up to what we read in "The Beatitudes." Therefore, you cannot separate "The Beatitudes" from the rest of Jesus' sermon. Blessed are the poor in spirit, the merciful, the pure in heart. You will be a light that shines in darkness only if you are measuring up to these things that Jesus listed in the beginning of His sermon. Then, as your light shines before men, they shall see your good works and thus glorify your Father which is in heaven.

Reference is also made to an individual who gives light unto all that are in the house. Jesus is talking about a candle that is placed in a candlestick. You are that candle. You are that light in your home and surroundings. You give light unto all that are in the house as you live the life of Christ, an example before the children and all others in that household. You are that light.

See something else here as we go back to that fourteenth verse and note that Jesus uses the word "city." I am not a city and neither are you a city. A city

118

is made up of many individuals; therefore, when Jesus speaks of a city, He is not talking about one person. What exactly does He mean? We all know that a city is made up of many people, so the city here refers to the Church. Jesus' Church should be a shining light, shining in all of its majestic splendor in this world of darkness. It should be as a great beacon where men and women who need salvation may come, where men and women seeking spiritual help may find an answer, and where those having a desire and a hunger to be delivered from their sins may find a new life in Christ. In this world of darkness, the Church should be as a shining beacon on a hill, towering over the wrecks of time, a place where people may come who desire to worship God. There they may enter the portals and find power and help and Jesus Christ, the One sufficient for all their needs.

My heart is burdened and I greatly fear that the light in some of God's cities is shining very dimly in this hour. The Church has lost much of its power, so much in fact that the hour has come when instead of beaming its light from the highest mountain peak and shining in majestic splendor, instead of challenging the world today, the world is challenging the Church. "God help us," is my prayer!

TEN

Heaven's Righteousness

Everything that Jesus said in the Sermon on the Mount applies to us today, and continues to be full of meaning until this hour. But, I am convinced that not one of us will be able to completely comprehend the full depth of its scope until we get home to glory. Yet we know that God honors our desire to discern His ways, and we know that the Holy Spirit anoints and unfolds and reveals God's truths to seeking hearts and minds.

Jesus, who understands the workings of the human mind, was aware that those who sat on the side of that hill were acquainted with the prophets. He knew the questions that His sermon spawned. People wondered whether these things that He was giving to them were in place of the Law, which they knew so well. They had been educated and schooled and taught to keep the Law; many were living according to the Law of Moses as best they could. Jesus perceived their thoughts that they were questioning whether His teaching would violate the Law or if it was to be a substitute for the Law.

Jesus quickly answered their questions with these words: "Think not that I am come to destroy the law, or the prophets: I am not come to destroy, but to fulfill" Matthew 5:17. Therefore, it is obvious that the Law and the Ten Commandments were not cancelled out or voided by the Sermon on the Mount. The Ten Commandments were meant to remain intact. Those ten laws are to govern man today in exactly the same way that they were designed by God to be a guide to His people when He gave them to Moses on Mount Sinai.

It is evident that we are living today in a different era or age. The Ten Commandments were given during the dispensation of God the Father, and we have already passed through the dispensation of Jesus Christ the Son. We are living now in the dispensation of the Holy Spirit, the third person of the Trinity. But the two dispensations preceding this one under the Holy Spirit were not cancelled out or voided. God's ten rules for living, therefore, remain in force and are just as effective today as they were for the children of Israel. They will continue to be in effect, continue to be active, until "all be fulfilled," as the Word of God states. Jesus made it very clear that He did not come to cancel out the Law. He came that through Him we can experience that divine new birth where one passes from death unto life and enters into the Kingdom of God. Then He sent the Holy Spirit, whose power and strength are imparted to us, making it possible for us to keep these laws. It is just that simple.

As a Christian, I tell you very frankly that I find myself having no struggle whatsoever in keeping the Ten

Commandments. I realize that they come from the very throne of God, from the very hand of the mighty Creator. These are the ten rules that He has given to humanity, and if they are not kept, there is a penalty for that man and that woman. But a Christian with Christ living in his heart, with newness of life generating power within him, automatically keeps the Ten Commandments without strain or stress. These rules are still there and remain in effect. They have never been cancelled or rescinded. But Christ, living within the heart of the born-again person, makes it possible for one to keep these commandments, until these rules become a natural way of life and living. In other words Jesus is saying, "In Me the law is fulfilled."

That isn't all. Let's go a little deeper. Jesus is about to say something that is vitally important, because whenever He uses the word "verily," it is a signal that prompts us to listen closely. Now if I would want to give special emphasis to something in my sermon, I would say to my listening audience: "Listen closely." But Jesus used just one word—verily—and whenever that single word was spoken, we need to pay heed and listen carefully.

"For verily I say unto you, Till heaven and earth pass, one jot or one tittle shall in no wise pass from the law, till all be fulfilled" (Matthew 5:18). In that one verse alone, we have enough prophecy, enough meat, enough deep truth that it would take hours to convey the full interpretation if one were to delve in and give the meaning in full and minute detail. I know it is common practice, when one comes to a Scripture that he does not fully understand, to say that it is a figure of speech—and then pass it by. But this is not a figure of speech that Jesus was using here. He was talking about a real heaven, and about this earth on which you and I live here and now. In substance, perfectly knowing both worlds—Heaven and Earth—He was saying that the Law cannot fail. The Law cannot be set aside. It cannot be ignored. It cannot be trifled with as something unimportant. While there is a Heaven above and as long as the Earth is in its present form, the law that God the Father gave cannot be trifled with as unimportant. It will remain in effect and will continue until all be fulfilled.

Now for just a moment, we are going to see exactly what Jesus meant when He said, "Till heaven and earth pass." This was not spoken carelessly or as a figure of speech. He meant what He said literally, and His statement was all-important or He would never have prefixed it with the word "verily." Heaven and earth shall pass, and this statement would supposedly prompt some to say, "I always did believe that the world is going to come to an end." If you believe that, however, you are wrong in your belief. The world will never come to an end. Then what did Jesus mean here as He said, "Till Heaven and Earth pass"?

Peter and John had the knowledge, so let us read what these men had to say. First of all, please turn to 2 Peter 3:13, "Nevertheless," Peter said, "we, according to his promise, look for new heavens and a new earth, wherein dwelleth righteousness." The Law that God himself gave continues. Those ten rules for man's living will continue in effect until, on this planet, there dwells perfect and complete righteousness. There will not be perfect righteousness on this planet, however, until this Earth, as it is in its current condition as we know it, shall pass away.

In other words, there will be a time when there will be absolute righteousness on this planet, and when we have absolute righteousness, we will have the ultimate law. But, even then, the Law as we know it will not be destroyed, but it will have passed from word to spirit, from cold letter into warm life. The Law as it is today and as it has always been, is cold letter. There is coming a day, however, when perfect and complete righteousness will be upon this planet, and then the cold letter will be turned into warm life. That seems simple, I know, but it is the best way I can explain it.

Now we are going to consider something a little different in regard to Jesus' words, "Till heaven and earth pass." It is fact that the place that we now call Heaven is only temporary. It is not eternal. If your loved one was a Christian and died in the Lord, the very minute his heart stopped beating, death came and the soul left that body and went into Heaven where Jesus is at this present time. We place that loved one's body in the grave, but the soul which is eternal, goes all the way from that body here on Earth into the place that we commonly call Heaven, into the presence of Jesus.

But Heaven, as we understand it today, is only a temporary place because Jesus will not always remain in the position and in the place which we call Heaven now. There is a place that will, in the future, be our eternal Heaven. The Apostle John saw it in a vision and it is recorded in Revelation 21:1, "And I saw a new heaven and a new earth: for the first heaven and the first earth were passed away." John saw the city of the new Jerusalem coming down to this Earth. Even Jesus, before He went away, said: "I go to prepare a place for you" (John 14:2). Work is now going on and the new Jerusalem is under construction. I do not believe for one minute that when we die, we will sit around, playing a harp, admiring our crowns and lounging idly by for eternity. I personally could not be happy sitting down doing nothing. That would be contrary to my nature and my disposition. I am convinced that there is great activity going on even now in the place that we call Heaven. Jesus said, "I go to prepare a place for you," and if one is preparing something, that one is working, and Jesus has His staff working hard on the city of the new Jerusalem. Just how and to what extent I cannot say, for that is not revealed in the Bible; but in John's vision, he saw the city coming down out of the heavens to this planet on which you and I live.

Perhaps you can see my point now. That is exactly what Jesus meant when He said, "Till heaven and earth pass"—until that which is temporary will pass away. But, the city of the new Jerusalem cannot come down on Earth in this planet's present state. Therefore, there must be a time when something happens to the surface of this planet. This world will never come to an end. The Bible does not teach that this planet will be destroyed. The surface will be destroyed and renovated by fire, and you can depend on God to do a good housecleaning and renovating job on this Earth one of these days. Not one thing will be left on the surface of this earth that was here while sin and the enemy of our soul reigned. This earth will be restored to its original beauty one day. And do you know why? Because God will never be defeated. He knows no defeat.

There was a time, you know, when the surface of this planet was beautiful. That which was once on the surface of the Earth we now find in the bowels of the earth, for God reached down in judgment one day and with His arm of wrath, turned this planet inside out.

That is the reason we have the minerals and the precious stones in the bowels of the earth today. That is the reason for the craters and the mountains.

There are many Scriptures to substantiate the fact that there was something on this Earth prior to the creation of man, for when God created Adam and Eve, He directed them to "*replenish* the earth" (Genesis 1:28). One cannot replenish something that was barren and void prior to that time. Therefore, we know that before Adam and Eve were placed on this Earth, there was life of some kind here; in God's purpose and plan, He made it possible that this planet would again be replenished and inhabited. This raises the question: What was here prior to Adam and Eve?

The other night I was watching television and a program came on that proved to be most interesting. Scientists have found positive proof of life on this earth millions of years ago. Now a skeptic will immediately say that such evidence is in conflict with what the Bible says—that the earth is six thousand years old. No, the Bible does not say that at all. It states that man is approximately six thousand years old, but this planet can be billions and billions and billions of years old and not contradict the Bible. God created man about six thousand years ago, but vegetation and other life were on this planet millions or even billions of years before that time. I believe that Lucifer, one of the three chief angels, ruled and reigned over thousands and thousands of angels on this planet before his fall. This planet was beautiful beyond description, and our poor puny minds cannot fathom the beauty of this earth before it was touched by sin. One day God is going to restore this same planet to its original beauty, and man, having accepted Christ as Savior, will rule and reign with Him in perfect righteousness on a perfect Earth.

Do you really comprehend what this means? God will repopulate this planet with free moral agency after it has been restored. Those of us who have been redeemed and who have freely chosen to accept Jesus as our Savior, Master, and Ruler, living the Christian life, will one day be a part of the new Heaven and new Earth. It will be then, and not until then, that righteousness will be the ultimate law. At that time, God's ten rules for living will have passed from word to spirit.

Read Matthew 5:19 now for yourself: "Whosoever therefore shall break one of these least commandments, and shall teach men so, he shall be called the least in the kingdom of heaven: but whosoever shall do and teach them, the same shall be called great in the kingdom of heaven."

What does Jesus mean here when He says: "Whosoever shall do and teach them"? He is speaking about the Law, God's ten rules for living, as they were given to Moses;

128

and we know that it has been proven that the only power of teaching is that of the doing which precedes it. It is absolutely impossible for any person to teach a commandment with power if he himself is breaking that commandment in his own life. That is the reason why I say you cannot give to anyone else any more than you have experienced yourself. This is the relation of His disciples to the Law: break the commandment and teach men so, and you are the least in the Kingdom. But on the other hand, do the commandment, be obedient to the commandment and teach men so, and you are great in the Kingdom. It is just that simple, simple enough that even a child can understand it.

Now look at Matthew 5:20, where Jesus once again reminds His listeners that He is the one that is doing the preaching: "I say unto you, That except your righteousness shall exceed the righteousness of the scribes and Pharisees, ye shall in no case enter into the kingdom of heaven." These are important words. Exactly what is the righteousness "that exceeds?"

Remember, the scribes and the Pharisees were sticklers for the Law, insomuch that they actually dared come into the presence of Jesus and accuse Him of breaking the Law. You will recall that Sabbath morning when Jesus and His disciples went through the corn fields. They were hungry and the Pharisees accused the Son of God of breaking the "Law of the Sabbath," because the disciples picked and ate the corn on the Sabbath. The scribes and Pharisees were sticklers for the Law, yet their own lives did not measure up to the Law. They preached it, but they did not live it. That is what prompted Jesus to say, "Except your righteousness shall exceed the righteousness of the scribes and the Pharisees, ye shall in no case enter into the kingdom of heaven." What then is the "righteousness that exceeds?"

It is apparent that the "righteousness that exceeds" is evidenced by both DOING and TEACHING. You are to DO and SAY, to BE and TEACH. The righteousness of the Pharisees was the righteousness that conditioned their external life only. It was an outward show. It can be likened to someone who never takes a bath getting all dressed up. The beautiful clothing was for outward show, but inside there was rottenness to the core.

The righteousness that Jesus demands is that which conditions the hidden and the internal, which is the heart and the soul. Sooner or later, if the inside of man is rotten, his deeds will also be rotten. The righteousness of the Pharisees can be labeled the righteousness that expresses itself in the correct outer garb, something holy for the eyes of men to behold. Jesus rebuked them and reminded them that their prayers did not reach any higher than the roof over their heads, because they prayed only for effect so that men might see them and that they might be heard of men.

Anything that you or I do to be seen of men, anything we do to get human approbation, anything that we do for effect is never acceptable before God. These things are no more than the shoddy righteousness of the scribes and the Pharisees. You may not like this kind of preaching, but it is time to take inventory and discover whether we have the right kind of righteousness.

The righteousness that exceeds does not begin with the keeping of the Law. The righteousness that exceeds is the righteousness that is anxious about righteousness, judgment, mercy, truth, all the weightier matters of the Law. Now, what does one do to get this righteousness that exceeds? In analysis, we have seen that the righteousness of the Pharisees was the righteousness conditioned by externals only, but Jesus came to condition the internal, and in so doing He took care of the externals as well.

God is perfect in all His ways. He works from within, and you are obedient to Him because you love Jesus Christ. You love others because of the new-birth that automatically clothes you with the righteousness of God in Christ Jesus (2 Corinthians 5:21).

ELEVEN

The Ultimate Law of God

I have reflected on this question, mulling it over in my mind again and again, and the only answer I can give is a very simple one: the ultimate Law of God is great love.

God's love for mankind was so great that He sent His own Son to correct the very root of our sin, and when we are governed by the living Christ who dwells within us, it becomes the most natural thing in the world to keep the cold, outward letter of the Law.

We will not steal or bear false witness, commit-murder, or sin in any way as long as we have love—God's love—in our hearts. Where there is no inner hatred, our deeds will be deeds of love and kindness.

The one in whose heart Jesus lives finds it easy to forgive, easy to be pure, easy to not murder or do any unkindness. Jesus did not come to destroy the Law as it was given to Moses, but to take us further than the Law could ever go.

The Law was written on cold tables of stone, but the ethics of Jesus are written in the hearts of those who are born again. The letter of the Law is cold and without heart or feeling, but the ultimate Law, the perfect law of righteousness, is established and reigns in the hearts of Christ's believers in whom He lives.

Beloved, the sin that curses society today is the sin of the heart, and only Jesus Christ, God's Son, holds in His hand the cure.

TWELVE

Protection of Angels

Happy are they that have eyes to see:
They shall find God everywhere;
They shall see Him where others see stone.
And happy are they who know the power of love;
They live in His Spirit for God is love.
Happy are they that live for truth:
They find a way to relieve the hearts of men;
And happy are the souls fully given to Thee;
They shall be filled with peace and perfect love.

God has made glorious provisions for His children; provisions to protect them, surround them, and provide for all their needs, and angels play a mighty important part in this plan of God's. They are busy creatures indeed. Never forget that you and I do not fight the battle of life alone. We are not walking our way alone, we are never alone day or night. Our Lord has made provision for us as His children to be protected.

Now the subject of angels is so prominent in the Scriptures that whenever I speak regarding the fact of angels and the ministry of angels, I feel most inadequate and am aware I cannot deal with it fully. But one cannot study the Word of God without realizing that angels are very real creatures, beings created by God long before the world as we know it was made. They have habitations, just as we have homes in which to dwell. They possess some form of a body like ours, having hands and feet, and they are able to eat, yet they differ from man in that angels have no spirit, since they are spirit.

I shall never forget the very first time I received light from the Word of God on the fact that angels eat. You see, as a child, I was led to believe that angels did little more than fly about to display their beautiful wings, and so more than anything else I wanted to be an angel with wings like theirs. I could not picture an angel eating food.

Yet, as I began to study the Word of God, I found that angels not only possess a body, they also eat, for in Genesis 18, angels were entertained by Abraham in his tent. They ate of the meat and the bread that he had prepared for them. Then, in delving deeper into God's Word, I found that angels have a very special kind of diet for the Bible speaks of angels' food in the Psalm 78:24-25. The author of this Psalm describes it as follows: "And [God] had rained down manna upon them to eat, and had given them of the corn of heaven. Man did eat angels' food: he sent them meat to the full."

If you have studied the account of the exodus of the children of Israel from Egypt, you know all about that wonderful manna that was sent fresh each morning from heaven for them to gather. They thrived on it. But do you fully realize that the manna they ate for forty years was really angels' food? God literally opened up the angels' breadbox for His people, and manna came down to them from heaven to feed them throughout their forty-year trek in the wilderness. And I sometimes wonder if we, too, shall have the opportunity to eat angels' food when we finally get to heaven. You may question why I say this, but you will understand if you will turn to Revelation 2:17. "To him that overcometh will I give to eat of the hidden manna." I admit that I am looking forward to partaking of that manna some day. Aren't you?

Let us go a little deeper into the ministry of angels, and here you will notice something else: God has no time for lazy creatures whether they are angels or people. God believes in work. First of all, go back to God's law for men and women, which states: "Six days shalt thou labour, and do all thy work" (Exodus 20:9). It was never God's plan that man should work only three or four or five days out of every week. God's Word reveals He expects us to work six days. Then we are instructed to come on the seventh day and rejoice and give praise unto the Giver of every good and perfect gift. So it is with angels. Angels have a ministry: they do not sit around and do nothing but enjoy themselves, for the Word of God says, "Are they not all ministering spirits, sent forth to minister for them who shall be heirs of salvation?" (Hebrews 1:14).

We have all watched little children at play, I'm sure, and have seen how near they come to danger. It is then that I am reminded of the Scripture in Matthew 18:10:

"Take heed that ye despise not one of these little ones; for I say unto you, That in heaven their angels do always behold the face of my Father which is in heaven." Were it not for the protective presence of angels, I wonder how many children would grow up to become adults.

Now Satan would destroy all of God's elect if he could, and if God would permit. But God has charged these angels with the responsibility of protecting His own. If He didn't, and if there were no provisions made for our protection throughout our lives, we would fall before Satan's onslaught as surely as we were born. And this ministry of angels continues during all our lives and all along the way.

Looking back, we have many examples of God's protective hand. We read in the Old Testament, when God's judgment was about to fall and destroy Sodom, that He made it known to Lot—by angels—in order that he and his family might escape the fire and brimstone (Genesis 19).

When Daniel was in the lion's den, confronted with an impossible situation, he was protected by angels. He stood without fear, knowing that he was not alone. There was no uncertainty in his heart concerning God's limitless power. He was void of frustration and nervousness. He had perfect trust and confidence in his Lord; God used angels to close the mouths of the lions, for he testified: "My God hath sent his angel, and hath shut the lions' mouths" (Daniel 6:22).

When the prophet Elisha was surrounded by the armies of Syria, you will remember that he prayed that

God would open the eyes of his servant. This servant could not see God's army encamped about them. He had no spiritual vision or knowledge of the Lord's protection in the heat of the battle. Not until the servant's spiritual eyes were opened did he behold the mountain filled with horses and chariots of fire, angels sent from heaven to protect them (2 Kings 6:17).

If only we could see that which Elisha saw, we too would be filled with wonder and courage at the marvelous sight; for I believe that as surely as God gave protection to Elisha and his servant, God protects His own this very hour. He is protecting you. He is protecting me. In this hour when worry is overcoming you and fear is gripping every part of your being, your fears would flee if only you could SEE the angelic hosts that surround you.

Turn to the New Testament where we read of Peter who was in prison (Acts 5 and Acts 12). It was an angel, sent by God, that came to deliver him in both instances, and we have Peter's testimony in Acts 5:19: "But the angel of the Lord by night opened the prison doors, and brought them forth."

I do not believe that the angel had to resort to picking the lock in order to open that prison door. No sir! He wasn't a safe-cracker! I believe he opened that door as easily as though the door had never been locked, and Peter knew what happened. A similar incident (Acts 12:5-10) took place later in the life of Peter when again an angel released him from prison. As I reread this Scripture I can imagine hearing the angel say: "Come on, Peter. Follow me. I'll show you the way out. Follow me and you will be all right."

Many times we have come close to disaster, an accident or some danger hovered near. Had it not been for the angel of the Lord protecting and guarding us, calamity surely would have occurred.

Protection is a real part of our inheritance as God's children. Angels are busy creatures in God's wonderful universe. They are never said to sleep or to rest, but are constantly active night and day. "The angel of the LORD encampeth round about them that fear him, and delivereth them" (Psalm 34:7). In God's plan for His children, there is more involved than any of us fully realize. Angels are ministering hosts, sent by God to protect us; they are encamped about those who love and fear Him and obey Him.

There may be times that you have been impressed to do something on the spur of the moment, not knowing exactly why you felt impressed to do it. That has happened to me, too. In such instances it is possible that we have been led by an angel of the Lord, sheltered or protected by an angel. There are times when doors have been wonderfully opened to us due to an angel's presence. It is possible that legions of angels have surrounded us at times, even as they surrounded Elisha and his servant on that day recounted in 2 Kings 6:17.

What a glorious and comforting thought it is to the believer, knowing that God has ordered His angels to not only protect, but also to deliver us in times of trouble. If we could only realize that the armies of heaven are truly at our disposal—if we could believe and know that the heavenly hosts are encamped about us, we would place far less confidence in the arm of flesh, less reliance upon physical weapons for our defense, and rest more certainly and securely in the power of our God. Sometimes I think we get so caught up in what is happening about us that we forget to lean on God. We try to fight our own battles, and then discover ourselves in a situation more desperate than the difficulty with which we started.

I challenge you at this very moment to cease leaning on your own devices and start leaning on the Lord. He will not only protect you, He will deliver you! He has ways and means of rescuing us in times of trouble that we never imagined. God's Word states that the weapons of our warfare are not to be carnal (2 Corinthians 10:4). They should never be carnal, but spiritual!

Right now, therefore, look up and say with assurance: "I, too, am one of God's precious children. If He gave protection to Elisha, He will give protection to me. If He stopped the lions' mouths for Daniel, He will do it for me. If He opened the prison door for Peter and led him to freedom, He will lead me out of my troubles and my material prison, too!"

Psalm 91 is very familiar to all Christians, I am sure. It is loaded with a list of God's benefits; therefore, let us pause here and read it together. If your mind is filled with fear at this moment, in the light of the promises in this Psalm, I remind you of the fact that there is no reason to be afraid. Dare to believe God's Word!

"He that dwelleth in the secret place of the most High shall abide under the shadow of the Almighty" (Psalm 91:1). This is the opener and herein lies the secret.

My question now is this: Are you abiding in God and does He abide in you? What is your relationship to Him? Where are you living? How are you living? If you do not possess a right relationship to God, the remainder of this Psalm is not yours to claim.

If your answer is "yes," however, then you can truly say: "I will say of the LORD, He is my refuge and my fortress: my God; in Him will I trust. Surely He shall deliver me from the snare of the fowler, and from the noisome pestilence. He shall cover me with His feathers, and under His wings shall I trust: His truth shall be my shield and buckler. I shall not be afraid for the terror by night; nor for the arrow that flies by day; nor for the pestilence that walks in darkness; nor for the destruction that wastes at noonday. A thousand shall fall at my side, and ten thousand at my right hand; but it shall not come nigh me. Only with my eyes shall I behold and see the reward of the wicked."

Why can we be assured of these blessings? Read on with me: "Because thou hast made the LORD, which is my refuge, even the most High, thy habitation; there shall no evil befall thee, neither shall any plague come nigh thy dwelling. For he shall give his angels charge over thee, to keep thee in all thy ways."

I ask you again: In view of these promises, where is there room for fear? Where is there cause for worry? Where is there place for anxiety and frustration if your trust and confidence are in God? The mighty Lord of this universe has said that because you have made Him your refuge and have made Him and His truths the place of your habitation, no trouble or plague outside of His perfect will shall befall you or come near your dwelling. And because He has made these provisions for His own, He gives His angels charge over you and me, to keep us in all our ways.

As marvelous as all of this is, there is more. The interest of angels goes deeper than our protection. Do you know they are interested in our redemption and our salvation? Let me remind you that angels can never personally experience the joy we know when Jesus becomes our Redeemer. You may wonder why, and it is because angels have no need of redemption. Angels can never know the thrill and the joy and peace that come into the life of an individual who has found salvation in Christ. Nevertheless, they are deeply interested in the plan of our salvation and our redemption. In 1 Peter 1:12, we are told that they desire to look into this great plan of salvation, and this fact speaks to us of the curiosity of the angels. And Jesus plainly tells us there is joy in the presence of the angels of God over one sinner that repents (Luke 15:7).

You and I may not know the supreme value of a soul, but the angels do. You and I may take for granted the conversion of a human being, but the angels comprehend the great miracle that takes place when the blood of Jesus cleanses from all sin. There are instances when we can see only a little outward display of emotion when that one accepts Christ as Savior, but I can assure you that there is great emotion and excitement and rejoicing among the angels in heaven as they witness such a miracle. This may surprise you as it did me when I first realized this fact, but it is because they know the value of one soul that repents.

Yes, I agree that all of this is wonderful, but that isn't all. To me the glorious climax, the grand finale of the entire ministry of heaven's angels, comes at the time when we need them most: at the moment when this mortal body takes its final breath. I know of no more comforting truth in the entire Bible concerning the angels, than their ministry to us in the hour of our death should we die before the Lord Jesus returns.

You see, when a saint dies, his soul and his spirit go directly into Heaven while his body is temporarily placed in the grave awaiting the resurrection of the physical at the return of Christ. In order for the spirit and soul of the saint to go into Heaven, it is necessary that they pass through the atmosphere, the air that surrounds this Earth. We know that the atmosphere surrounding our Earth is the particular abode of Satan and his fallen angels, for Satan is described in the Scriptures as "the prince of the power of the air" (Ephesians 2:2). And these fallen angels are traditional enemies of not only Christ but all that belong to Him. We may, therefore, logically expect that the passage of a saint at death from Earth to Heaven would be vigorously contested by Satan and by his angels, because it is their last and final opportunity to attack the believer on his journey home.

Were it not for the promises of God, therefore, it is possible that the saint may never reach Heaven; but God has made glorious provision for this as well. There is a special army, a host of angels, whose particular duty is to bring the souls of God's people at the time of their death into their heavenly home, and into the very presence of the Savior. To me this is one of the angels' most thrilling assignments.

If you are a Christian, you need not worry about a thing. Stop fretting about a roof over your head and things that do not amount to a hill of beans. Stop worrying about death. Our heavenly Father has not forgotten a thing! I know the fears you face, I encounter them, too. But I have learned that after I have covered all bases and have done my homework to the best of my ability, God will take over and supply where I am lacking. He is in control and He has not only thought about all the details providing for my spiritual needs and all my material things while here on Earth, but He has made dead sure that I shall arrive in Heaven safely, protected all the way. And He will do it for you as well!

Notice in Luke 16:22: "And it came to pass, that the beggar [Lazarus] died, and was carried by the angels into Abraham's bosom." The Word of God does not state that he was escorted by angels, but CARRIED by the angels into Abraham's bosom. Lazarus was carried! What an experience that must have been, and what an experience it will be for all of God's home-going saints! It almost causes one to long for death and that thrilling reality of being carried by Heaven's angels into the presence of God. Without doubt, it takes the fear out of dying—death becomes a glorious climax to a life lived for God, instead of a dreaded foe.

The world's champions are honored and toasted when they return home after winning a victory. The crowds are waiting, the flags are waving, ticker tape and confetti fill the air as the great conqueror parades in a special car along with other dignitaries, surrounded by secret police and a great array of military.

But, beloved, that is as nothing compared to the glory and thrill that is the portion of the believing Christian who goes home, who leaves this body of clay, is loosed from this old Earth; marking the end to all tears, to all sufferings, and to all disappointments. We need not fear or dread death. To the Christian, death means leaving behind him all the sham, and leaving all the hurts that have caused sorrow. Death is to go home surrounded by a heavenly host, carried by God's angels into His own wonderful presence. It is joy unspeakable. "O death, where is thy sting? O grave, where is thy victory?" (1 Corinthians 15:55).

Confidence in God and trust in the heavenly Father will take away all sting of death. We can confidently say with David: "Yea, though I walk though the valley of the shadow of death, I will fear no evil: for thou art with me; thy rod and thy staff they comfort me" (Psalm 23:4).

You are not alone today, and your heavenly Father will not leave you alone tomorrow. He will be with you in life to the very end, and on that final day when this mortal life is over, angels will tenderly carry you into the presence of your Lord and God. That is what it means to be a Christian.

THIRTEEN

Balancing of the Clouds

If you have spent many hours in the air like I have, looking out from your seat in an airplane flying through the clouds, you may understand why I felt it was not just a happenstance when I opened my Bible during a flight to California and read that glorious scripture found in the thirty-seventh chapter of Job, the sixteenth verse: "Dost thou know the balancings of the clouds, the wondrous works of him which is perfect in knowledge?"

Sometimes those clouds may be filled with rain, but what a comfort it is to know that no strange hand has veiled our sky. It is the most wonderful thing in the world, it is the greatest security that a human being can experience, to know that whether we are sailing through clouds and our day is dark, whether the rain is falling or the sun is shining, regardless of circumstances or conditions that face us, no strange hand has veiled our sky.

Yes, the shadows may have gathered, but they have gathered at the will of Him who we trust. If you are God's child; if you are living in the very center of His will; if you have committed unto Him body, soul and spirit; if you have come to the place in your consecration where you literally have no will of your own, and you have completely turned your life and your will over to Him, and you are guided by His hand, then not one sorrow has befallen you—or can befall you in the future—save by His appointing and for the fulfillment of His merciful purpose.

Sometimes we are too blind, too feeble, to understand the balancing of the clouds and the wondrous works of Him who is perfect in knowledge. But we know that His name is love, and behind all the mystery is the light that changes not. When we face the balancing of the clouds, it is the wondrous work of Him who is perfect knowledge and perfect wisdom. We cannot always understand, but one thing I discovered a long time ago: Sore trials make common Christians into uncommon saints, and make them fit for being used for uncommon service. It matters not who you may be. You may consider yourself the most common and ordinary person in the world, but God can take that life of yours and change it into one of the most beautiful, and make of you an uncommon saint. And when He has made you into an uncommon saint, He will use you in an uncommon service. You have heard me say it over and over again, I'm sure: It isn't silver or golden vessels God seeks, but yielded vessels. And sometimes, when those clouds are thick and dark and the storm comes, it isn't the easiest thing to continue to yield to the One who has perfect knowledge; but we must trust Him with a perfect trust and a perfect confidence.

Perhaps this analogy will help you to understand what I am trying to say. I have a few plants on my outside patio and one is especially beautiful. I have watched it bud, and have seen it come to full bloom. Then the storm and the rains came and that blossom that was so lovely suddenly dropped its head in the pitiless storm. It appeared that all its glory, all its beauty was gone. The night passed and morning came and the sun shone again bringing light and strength to the flower. When I looked at it again, its head was held high and its petals were open. Not only had it regained its glory, but it seemed more beautiful than before. This fragile blossom coming in contact with the fierce storm seemed to be a defeated thing. But, as it came in contact with a stronger force than the storm, it received strength and its beauty was not only restored but was even greater.

I cannot tell you how it is possible that I should be able to receive into my being a power to do that which is greater than my own ability or strength or might. But it is a fact. I know that I need not be defeated on a single score. I can tell you of a truth, and I will stake my life on it: You do not have to be defeated on a single score IF you will make contact with the Holy Spirit. It matters not how great your storm or the density or darkness of the clouds through which you are passing. We speak of the great compassion of the Lord Jesus Christ, and God's mercy and His fathomless love. But, you and I cannot live and know victory without the fellowship and the communion with the Holy Spirit. There—in Him—lies our secret of strength and victory. The great Apostle Paul could not have lived victoriously, he could not have survived those storms that threatened his very life, he could not have gone through his testing times triumphantly had it not been for the power of the Holy Spirit.

"Dost thou know the balancings of the clouds?" Over and over again you have heard me say: life is a balance. It is never unlimited joy. Yet, there are people who think that life should be constant pleasure, that every day should be a glorious picnic. If you are a part of humanity, there will be sorrows and disappointments. There will be tragedy. But God sees to it that there will be the balancing of the clouds. As surely as there is a cloud, there also will be the sun, and you can always know that God will balance the clouds for He is perfect in knowledge.

Your responsibility is not the balancing of the clouds in your life. Your part and mine is how we face those clouds and what we do with our sorrows and disappointments. If it was in our power to balance the clouds, we would have every day filled with beautiful sunshine. We would have the temperature just right— never too cold and never too hot. We do not control the weather and neither can we balance the clouds. No man can. God alone knows exactly HOW to balance those clouds. The only thing that you and I have to worry about is what we do with that tragedy, what we do with that suffering and that sorrow and those disappointments when they come.

You will recall that the Lord commissioned Joshua after the death of Moses to lead the children of Israel into the Promised Land. This great hero, Joshua, not without human weaknesses, must have had his fears for the Lord spoke to him in these words: "Be strong and of a good courage; be not afraid, neither be thou dismayed: for the LORD thy God is with thee whithersoever thou goest" (Joshua 1:9). Surely these are among the most reassuring and the most meaningful words ever spoken.

So it is with you. Once you have heard God's teaching and have realized that you are His child, and have put your trust in Him—once you have accepted the necessity of having faith in Him and His promises, then it is that you are able to lay hold of the courage you need for facing life. You must have courage to face life today. But "HOW?" is the question. We must face the future and all the problems of tomorrow with courage in the One who is perfect wisdom and perfect knowledge. And do not fail to recognize that the courage to live well needs a clean foundation.

I believe we should also bear in mind that one cannot be a person of courage and, at the same time, live a soft life. I hope I can make myself clear on this point. Courage must be exercised in your life or you will find you no longer possess it. There is nothing in the Scriptures, nor in human experience, to indicate that we can safely permit ourselves to get soft.

Sometimes I feel that is what is wrong with the generation in which we are living. The generation of today is not what you would call the sturdiest that ever lived. We must be very careful to shy away from the tendency to assume that it is good to have an easy life. Today too many seem to look for the easy way out and an easy life. I'll never forget the father who came to me recently and vowed: "My son and my daughter will never have to go through what I went through when I was their age. No! I was born poor. We didn't have two nickels to rub together. I got up at four o'clock each morning to chop wood. I had to walk five miles to go to school and it was plenty cold during the snowy wintertime. I had to work after school and on Saturdays all through my boyhood. But my son is not going to have to go through any of that. I will never have a child of mine face what I have been through."

Now that father's philosophy to spare his children the hardships he knew is likely to do his children a great disservice. Hardship and difficulty make strong men and women! The tough things that you have to face in life are really what make you a strong and a mature adult. Of course, you do not consider these things as stepping stones when you go through them. In reality, however, a person should thank the Lord for the tough things that come his way. I can look back now and thank God for every stone that ever bruised my feet. And when you can sincerely do that, you are making real progress in wisdom. The people who distinguish themselves in human life and rise to significant achievements, those who experience the greatest joys and the most satisfying victories, are those who accept difficulty as a challenge and do not let it frighten them.

Whatever you do, do not let difficulty or those clouds bring defeat to your life. "Dost thou know the balancings of the clouds, the wondrous works of him which is perfect in knowledge?" Allow God to balance the clouds, and remember that it is your responsibility and your part to trust Him!

Other Books by Kathryn Kuhlman
from Bridge-Logos

Glimpse Into Glory
The Greatest Power in the World
Heart to Heart
Never Too Late
Twilight and Dawn

The "Miracle Set:"
I Believe in Miracles
God Can Do It Again
Nothing Is Imossible With God

and the Only Authorized Biography
Daughter of Destiny
by Jamie Buckingham

The SPIRIT-FILLED CLASSICS Collection

This inspiring collection includes biographies of famous men and women who operated in the Gifts of the Spirit as well as time-honored works by these influential figures.

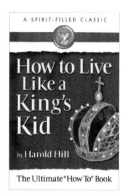

The Ultimate "How To" Book

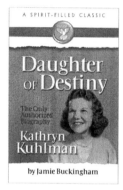

by Jamie Buckingham

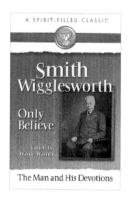

The Man and His Devotions

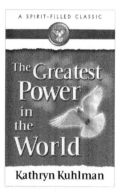

Kathryn Kuhlman

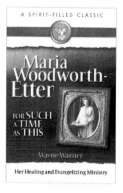

Her Healing and Evangelizing Ministry

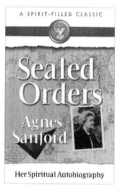

Her Spiritual Autobiography

His Life, His Teachings, His Influence

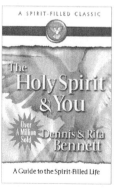

A Guide to the Spirit-Filled Life

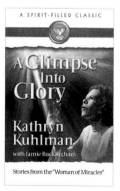

Stories from the "Woman of Miracles"

AVAILABLE AT FINE CHRISTIAN BOOKSTORES